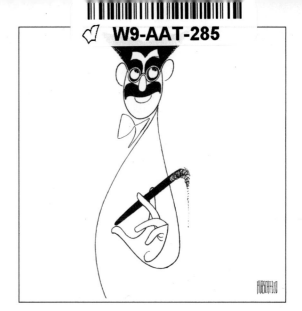

HIRSCHFELD'S IMMORTAL FRIARS

Front Endsheet: Top Row: *Eubie Blake, Irving Berlin, Jimmy Durante, Jack Benny, Groucho Marx*
                   Center Row: *George M. Cohan, Milton Berle, Humphrey Bogart, Sophie Tucker, William B. Williams*
                   Bottom Row: *Margo Feiden, Phil Silvers, Sammy Davis, Jr., Lionel Hampton, Steve Allen*

Back Endsheet: Top Row: *Bill Robinson, Bing Crosby, Lucille Ball & Desi Arnaz, Anthony Quinn, Bob Hope*
                   Center Row: *Will Rogers, Edward R. Murrow, Eddie Cantor, George Burns, Buddy Hackett*
                   Bottom Row: *Al Hirschfeld, George Gershwin, Joe DiMaggio, Frank Sinatra, Ed Sullivan*

A HUNDRED YEARS A MILLION LAUGHS

FRIARS CLUB

A CENTENNIAL CELEBRATION

BY BARRY DOUGHERTY

FOREWORD BY RICHARD LEWIS

For further information, contact the publisher at

Emmis Books
1700 Madison Road
Cincinnati, Ohio 45206
www.emmisbooks.com

ISBN 1-57860-161-4

LCCN 2004105793

Cover and interior designed by Patricia Prather, Dean Johnson Design
Edited by Jack Heffron

This book is dedicated to the longest-running joke in history.

May its punch line bring laughter to last till the end of time . . .

HERE'S TO THE FRIARS!

CONTENTS

FOREWORD

by Richard Lewis (AKA) "The Prince of Pain"

My name is Richard Lewis and I'm a proud, recovering alcoholic. I'm also an extraordinarily proud member of the Friars Club. There's no connection, other than the downside of the former, my sobriety, which thankfully has rid me of my drinking but has been replaced by close to one hundred thousand cross-addictions. For example, this is the four hundredth foreword for upcoming books that I have graciously written today. Being a sober mental case may not be the greatest attribute in turning my life around, but it was certainly instrumental in helping me become funnier and more honest on stage as a comedian and more truthful as a human being, an actor, and a writer. Also, these positives, thank God, enabled me to become the best Friar I can be.

Believe me, never in my wildest dreams, hellbent to make it in the arts as a comedian, did I think I would ever come close to feeling comfortable in my tragic, self-effacing skin and become a member of this legendary association. It is the most devoted and dedicated society to both the golden days and the up-to-the-minute show-business goings-on. Moreover, never, ever, as a Jew, could I imagine feeling as if I were born to hang out in a monastery.

For the record, I'm not taking on this illustrious writing endeavor for bread. Let's face it, giving blood is a gold mine next to this freebie. But who cares? I'm beyond elated for having been given the honor of writing the foreword for this magnificent book. *A Hundred Years, A Million Laughs* succeeds perfectly in documenting both with words and mesmerizing, pictorial imagery, one of the most beloved and significant historical American entertainment institutions. It's full of wondrous tales of gossip, glamour, laughs, and legends.

It exemplifies the underlying affection of the members (including yours truly) who have dedicated their lives to entertaining the world and affording people the luxury of forgetting their own personal travails. Most members, many of whom are considered world-renowned geniuses (that wouldn't be me, of course, unless you ask my girlfriend or people I lent money to) are sadly not only masters of their craft but are generally twisted, narcissistic, and for what it's worth, practically impossible to please when they are famished. (Fortunately, the food at the club is world renowned too.) And yet, even with their eccentricities, they remain the hippest, funniest, most compassionate people (other than the five members I want nothing to do with) that I have ever known. Unfortunately, as a Friar, I must also take into account their despicable table manners and nightmarish repetition of tales about their sexual encounters and scandalous rumors about the most famous people who ever lived. Mr. Dougherty brilliantly yet unscrupulously documents this legacy of memories that people have long begged to be privy to. He is an author with chutzpah and has an obvious flair for writing a bestseller without a twinge of guilt.

So without even the slightest grandiosity, I admit to being tremendously warped myself and more dysfunctional than total populations of most small countries. I certainly have paid my financial and psychological dues, in more ways than one, to be an upstanding and well-respected member of this social establishment and, with hope, will be proudly ridiculed in this masterwork as a reward.

Heading into its second century, the Friars Club has had many homes—clubhouses, if you will—and now the *monastery,* its affectionate nickname. This location has been its home since Uncle Miltie spearheaded the move to our almost surreally beautiful, English Renaissance townhouse on East 55th Street in Manhattan. And now, finally, after 'a hundred years and a million laughs' from the days and likes of Caruso, Cohan, Herbert, Berlin, Hammerstein, Rogers, and Fairbanks through the Rat Pack and Berle, Benny, and Burns up to the present-day personalities, we can have our very own private table. We can eavesdrop on all of these amazing anecdotes so rich and so much a part of the authentic fabric of our country told through numerous interviews and a seemingly endless number of astonishing photographs. The secrets are out, *"ladies and germs,"* and finally open to the public to see and hear the real dirt behind the infamous Roasts, testimonials and musings from the Friars who lived, and still live, this rich history. Rumor has it that even some deceased Friars have come back from their graves to help make this work of art the masterpiece it turned out to be, as long as the living Friars bought them lunch. Henny Youngman and I had a blast. He *still* found a fly in his soup.

The press agents from the turn of the century who created the club would be proud. The legends keep growing and the lies, truths, and boasts have never sounded more exhilarating or entertaining. This is a mind-blowing, must-see and must-read coffee-table book for anyone who ever dared to be entertained and who loves the rich history of magical talents who shared their affection and the fellowship of the Friars' spirit.

My only hope for myself, aside from getting my cholesterol down from ten thousand, is to continue to create and entertain all of you so I can always feel worthy of being a Friar. This foreword is now officially ending, the curtain is going up, and the show must go on! Have a blast! Oh, and if there is anything crazy said about me it's probably true. So I beg you to cut me a little slack. I'm only human—my biggest flaw. Besides, any Friar worth his salt has to have a few catastrophes and dark sides or he or she should immediately be blacklisted from the club, show business, and for sure, this wonderfully written legacy of love and lunacy.

ACKNOWLEDGMENTS

It's not easy writing a story that has been a hundred years in the telling but, man, has it been a fun ride. It's a given that a place known for its bawdy events and court jester-like characters is not going to have pristine records of their every moment from 1904 to 2004. As a matter of fact, they barely have a record of what happened an hour ago. Which is why piecing together this century-old jigsaw puzzle has been an amazing journey. To fit the pieces in place I talked to the most fascinating people who have the most interesting stories of eras gone by. Story by story and anecdote by anecdote the history of this amazing, albeit wacky, club became more and more mesmerizing, culminating in vivid accounts of a century of a wonderful place.

To this remarkable cross-generation of Friars who took the time to sit with me as I pried memories out of them—some of them decades old—I owe a tremendous debt of gratitude: Lucie Arnaz, Joy Behar, Carol Burnett, Red Buttons, Frank Capitelli, Buddy Clarke, Cy Coleman, Pat Cooper, Norm Crosby, Harry Delf, Jr., Phyllis Diller, Susie Essman, Judy Gold, Jack L. Green, Hugh Hefner, Bernie Kamber, Alan King, Susan Lucci, Ed McMahon, Jan Murray, LeRoy Neiman, David Hyde Pierce, Sally Jessy Raphael, Rob Reiner, Don Rickles, Joan Rivers, Freddie Roman, Jeffrey Ross, Neil Sedaka, Tom Smothers, Jerry Stiller, Stewie Stone, Barbra Streisand, and John Travolta. While some may have had more to say than others, every single comment made the Friars Club seem all the more endearing.

To Buddy Arnold, who passed away while this book was being written, I tip my hat skyward. I'm thankful I had the opportunity to listen to his fun stories of the early days with Milton Berle and put them down on paper so the Friars can pass on the legacy of a fascinating time in the history of their club. I also thank Berle for words he gave me before he died that still echo in my ears, some of which I was able to share. He was a giant in many ways and holds an esteemed place in the Friars record book.

What can I say about Richard Lewis that hasn't been discussed among psychotherapists in conventions around the world? Thank you, Richard, for penning your own passion for the Friars in the foreword and for sharing your personal experiences at the monastery with me. My head is still spinning but it's a good spin and my doctor tells me that my fits of laughter from talking with Richard should subside any day now. But I'm in no rush.

To Jean-Pierre Trebot, my fearless leader: *merci beaucoup*. This book has been a vision of his for almost a decade and I am grateful he has entrusted it to me. His confidence in my putting a hundred years of the Friars Club's memories into a book is to be commended. Or perhaps he should ask Richard Lewis for the name of a good shrink. I thank him for believing in me to pull this off. He will also be receiving the bill for my Valium prescription.

To the late radio personality Bob Fitzsimmons, who never lived to see his dream of the Friars archives compiled into a book for all to see—look at us now!

There are a few people who so kindly approached me with various artifacts or stories, puzzle pieces if you will, that have greatly helped in this tale of the Friars: Phil Agisim, who came upon the wonderful David Warfield dinner program; Mark Baren for locating a long-lost journal from the Friars Frolic of 1916 and giving it up for the Friars; Joan Cunningham, who shared her father Joe Cunningham's Friarly moments and helped to fill in a huge gap during the Friars lean years in the early '30s; Fred Tarter, who came across some wonderful Friars Club relics and chose to contribute them to the archives instead of making a killing on eBay; Bill Gulino, who contributed Milton Berle's bachelor dinner photo so everyone can now see Berle sweating in front of his future father-in-law; Thank you all for your loyalty and dedication to your club.

To Paul Rigby, who graciously allowed me to use his *New York Post* cartoon marking the Friars "Women in the Monastery" milestone and to Margo Feiden who oversees Al Hirschfeld's wonderful drawings from her Margo Feiden Galleries— thank you both for your artistic contributions.

To June Clark, my agent, and Jack Heffron, my editor, what can I say? Except, "You want me to write what when? Are you both out of your minds?" Thank you for your efforts in making this project actually happen.

I'm telling you now, I can't do it all! But what I can do is get some very talented people to help me. So thank you Alison Grambs and Shannon Skelley for transcribing hours of interviews—free hearing tests for both of you! To Erica Pearlstein, who let her fingers do the walking through Google and other websites to fill in the history gaps—thanks! To Eve Burhenne, who should be writing *Jeopardy* questions with the knowledge she possesses—I thank you for enduring my emails and phone calls and manic last-minute research requests.

The Friars have amassed thousands of photos over the last century, wonderful moments frozen in time that we are thrilled to put in this book. Thank you to some of the photographers who captured the Friars in the best of times: Michael Caputo (who, as the Friars Club's Assistant Executive Director, wears many more important hats than just photographer), Gene Gabelli, Richard Lewin, Bill Mark, Larry Rubino, Paul Schumach, and Sam Siegel. These few are just the tip of the iceberg, so to those early photographers who stood under blankets straddling old-fashioned camera contraptions on wooden tripods with exploding flashes—thanks.

Oscar Riba and Richard Lewin brought the Friars photo archives into the new millennium by scanning and organizing them all—thank you. If it were left to my resources, I would just paste them into every book individually.

A salute to the Friars Club staff, past and present (yes, even that bartender who sued the club in 1932) who have served the Friars loyally and had a great time in the process. They can all lay claim to "having the best job ever!"

To all the Friars who have ever walked through those monastery doors I thank you most of all for giving us one hundred years of sheer, unadulterated entertainment—this century was a blast!

—Barry Dougherty

CHAPTER ONE

PRESS AGENTS TO SUPERSTARS

The First Fifty Years

*All the world's a stage
and all the men and women, merely players.
They have their exits and their entrances,
and each one in their time plays many parts.*
—William Shakespeare

Above: *Program cover of the Friars
Oscar Hammerstein dinner — 1908*
Opposite page: *Friars Club's Oscar
Hammerstein dinner — 1908*

No institution has embraced Shakespeare's observation with as much unbridled bravado as the Friars Club. The Friars have parlayed one hundred years of antics into a reputation that has been elevated to legendary status. Since 1904, the Friars Club has been wining and dining the top personalities of the times and in between courses expounding and discoursing in their own unique fashion. From ribald comedy to musical merrymaking the Friars have spent a century cultivating a tradition that has spanned several generations and spawned millions of laughs.

The story of the Friars has been retold and retooled and revised so often that even Shakespeare's head would be spinning over the varied principle players, not to mention entrances and exits. But alas, he too would come to the same

The Friars

COMPLIMENTARY DINNER TO

OSCAR HAMMERSTEIN

ASTOR   DECEMBER 13, 1908.

PHOTO DRUCKER & Co, 200 W 43rd St, N.Y.

conclusion as the Friars did—who cares? Just sit back and enjoy the show, a show mind you, that has lasted one hundred years—even Broadway's *Cats* can't make that claim.

The beauty of the Friars Club is that the stories of its history are far more riveting than the actual facts. Take for instance Alan King's version. The comedian/film star holds the distinction of being the current abbot of the Friars Club. That's akin to being the chairman of the board for any non-entertainer types who are wondering if Alan has replaced his holiday Manischewitz with bottled wine spritzers. He's not heading for Rome, but he

Friars Frolic program featuring George M. Cohan on its cover—1916

is the big mucky muck at the Friars.

King's account (which admittedly is so much more entertaining when told from a Friars Club barstool) suggests that legendary George M. Cohan started the club for his equally famous father. It seems Jerry Cohan loved to drink, and before the Friars Club existed Jerry and George belonged to the Lambs Club. The Lambs was a popular private social club made up of fun-loving entertainers. One day Jerry got into a heated argument with the bartender and smashed every glass behind the bar. Needless to say, he was thrown out of the Lambs Club.

The man was beside himself, having lost his favorite watering hole. His son George begged the Lambs to reconsider, and his father was reinstated. On Jerry's first day back, while hanging out at the bar, a fellow Lamb asked Jerry what happened, that he hadn't seen him around the club. When Jerry said he was on suspension, his associate asked why. Jerry said, "This!" and proceeded to smash all the glasses again with his cane. What's a good son to do when his father is thrown out for good? Start a new club so Jerry could break glasses all day long. That club was the Friars!

GETTING STARTED

As much as the Friars love the story about the Cohans, the truth is that the club started with a group of press agents. Yes, it's a zzzzz's-rated story, to be sure. In any case, in 1904 eleven press agents got together to talk about people pretending to be members of the press just so they could get free tickets to Broadway shows. For the record the agents were: Charles Emerson Cook, Channing Pollock, John S. Flaherty, John B. Reynolds, John Rumsey, Philip Mindil, Mason Peters, William Raymond Sill, Burton Emmett, Bronson Douglas,

Cartoonist Ryan Walker's Friars Club dinner in their first clubhouse, which they referred to as the "friary"—1909.

Left: *Ryan Walker's illustrations of people around the friary—1909.*

and Harry Schwab. They are all the Friars Club's founding fathers, but if you ask any Friar today he or she will most likely tell you the club was started by George M. Cohan or Milton Berle, which is not a bad answer but not the correct one either.

After several meetings at Browne's Chophouse, and presumably a few rounds of the finest gin New York City offered, two very good things came out of the situation. One is that the press agents solved the fraudulent reporter problem by blacklisting the offenders; the other, more monumental, was that

they decided to keep on meeting once a week—just because. Hey, they liked each other, so go figure.

The year 1904 was a banner one in these United States. For the first time ever the Olympics were held on American soil, and the games were staged in connection with the World's Fair in St. Louis; the ice cream cone was invented; Times Square was created; work began on the Panama Canal; the New York City subway opened; the first flat-disk phonograph was introduced; the Rolls

Royce Company was founded; the first performance of J.M.Barrie's *Peter Pan* hit the stage; Helen Keller graduated from Radcliffe; and, especially delightful for the Friars Club, it is also rumored to be the year the comic book was invented. Oh hell, what didn't happen in 1904? It figures the Friars would somehow manage to squeeze in their own legacy among these historic gems.

Nothing personal to press agents, but the club didn't have a whole lot of pizzazz when it was called by its original name, the Press Agents Association. When the entertainers started palling around with them the name also didn't make a whole lot of sense, hence the change to the "Friars Club." Leave it to entertainers to stir things up. The name stems from the Latin "*frater*" meaning "brother." This alone solidified their mission— they would always be known as an entertainment fraternal organization, and the name said it all about their relationship to each other.

Why they opted for monastic terms is beyond anyone at this point, but their foresight for irony is uncanny. The head of the club they deemed "abbot," they called the president "dean," and other officers were "prior" and "scribe." A few years later they would even call their clubhouses "the friary" and "the monastery." When they later became known for their bawdy Roasts and ribald activities the inside joke was not lost on the savvy Friars.

Even the club's Latin motto, "*Prae Omnia Fraternitas,*" sounds like something a Benedictine monk should be canting from an altar on Sunday mornings. It translates to "Before All Things Brotherhood," but what really comes before brotherhood at the Friars is taking your best shot at an innocent ego and a slug of whiskey—but it's all good.

THE RIBALDRY BEGINS

It didn't take long for the Friars to discover they had the right stuff when it came to entertaining. Since they didn't have a clubhouse they could call their own yet, and chophouses and bars weren't terribly comfortable when they all brought their friends along for a good time, they began to hold lavish black-tie dinners in fancy locales. They would select a guest of honor and treat him to the finest night of his life with accolades and testimonials by various celebrity guests.

The first dinner of note was in 1907, which was the same year they officially incorporated, and honored Victor Herbert. He was a superstar of the day having composed such comic operettas as the popular *Babes in Toyland*. Every guest of honor makes a speech at the end of the event and Herbert's ranks among the most impressive Friars after-dinner speeches. Yes, even after all these years. Being a famed composer, he had at his disposal the tools to set to music his thoughts of the event. With the help of founding father and fellow Friar Charles Emerson Cook, who penned the words, Herbert wrote the song "Here's to the Friars," which became the Friars anthem. What is amazing is that the song continues to this day to hold that esteemed position. Unfortunately, it's sort of the "Star-Spangled Banner" of the Friars— revered by all but damned if anybody can ever remember the convoluted words.

Right at the outset the Friars got down and dirty. In spite of the sophistication that comes with donning a tuxedo, it seems the Friars also needed to don tough hides. As early as 1910 the Friars unorthodox treatment of their brethren garnered headlines. "FRIARS KID MR. HARRIS: Veteran Theatrical Manager Butt of Jokes at Dinner," blared the December 10, 1910 issue of the *New*

York Tribune the day after the Friars honored William Harris. Of course, the printed comments reflect the propriety of the times, but they do speak volumes about the Friars' acid tongues. "His record speaks for itself and, personally, I wish it had the lockjaw," intoned one speaker at the dinner. This comment, somewhat innocuous by modern standards, remains a cutting precursor to the official Roast jokes. For its day it was jarring enough to warrant commentary in the *Tribune* article: "When a man subjects himself to being honored at the hands of the Friars he needs a steel corselet to repel the jabs of his kidders."

Red Buttons is up to speed on how the Friars progressed from reserved to ribald: "I'll give you the analogy. Burlesque at one time was a family show. You bring your whole family to it. And then the women started working loose. Started cheating, started taking off more. When they did that the comedians tried to catch up with it. See, you can't follow that with Howdy Doody. You can't have somebody out there flashing a nipple or pubic hair or something like that and then walking out there and saying 'gosh' and 'darn.' So that was the evolution. It was like a cocoon. It became a war of attrition, they got a little loose, the comics followed suit, so before you know it, burlesque became double entendre at best, and I'm putting it mildly.

"And so the same thing happened with the dinners, not even the stag Roasts, the dinners, because the culture changed, women were liberated. You could say 'fuck' in company and nobody was going to throw you out on your rear anymore. People became liberated in the language, so that led to a breakdown in moralistic talk. The ethics were changing. So nobody said, 'Oh my God, did you hear what he said?' Today, even at the big dinners with the men and the women, somebody will say 'fuck'

Program for the Victor Herbert dinner — 1907

and it's nothing, it's part of the lexicon, that's it."

By the time 2000 came around, Rob Reiner was roasted by the Friars with comments such as this from Alan King: "His balls are bald, which gives truth to the adage that grass never grows on a busy street." That "steel corselet" has been replaced by a steel codpiece. But the intent remains the same and proof that such eloquence in a personal testimonial is inherent in the Friars gene pool. As a salve to heal the guest of honor's wounded pride, the Friars do offer up their motto, "We only roast the ones we love," and it's bought hook, line, and sinker.

But there are sweet memories, too, of Friars events, such as Susan Lucci's special moment at the Dean Martin testimonial dinner in 1984 that was held at the Waldorf Hotel. The queen of daytime TV recalls: "I remember being just thrilled to be included. When I got there it was even more thrilling because there were so many of the great entertainers there who I idolized, like Sammy Davis, Jr. and Dean Martin, and Shirley MacLaine. My dad loves redheads and always did, my mother's a redhead, and Shirley MacLaine was just high priestess in our house. That was his ideal, and to meet her then was wonderful. Frank Sinatra—this was incredible that I had the chance to meet him.

"When I walked into the reception before we went into the dinner I was bowled over by who I was seeing, and suddenly Sammy Davis, Jr. seemed to be walking in my direction. I did one of those things where I looked behind me to see who he was going to go and visit, and as he got closer it became clear that he was making eye contact with me, which I couldn't believe. He did, in fact, come over and introduce himself. He said that he really loved my work, and I'll never forget that as long as I live. That Sammy Davis, Jr. would know I was alive on the planet let alone be someone who watched me. He was so warm and charming, and he asked if I'd like to meet Frank Sinatra and Dean Martin. Of course, I was breathless.

"Then, going into the grand ballroom to sit on the dais, there was Lucille Ball in front of me and Milton Berle and all of these luminaries. Sammy

The Friars first clubhouse— 1908

Davis, Jr. brought the house down when he sang; and Red Buttons brought the house down. He was in rare form and everyone was doubled over and gave a standing ovation. I sat there thinking, my God, how lucky was I to be there that night with all of the greats. I was just in heaven." So it's not just about the dirty jokes.

FINDING A HOME

The early Friars didn't even have a home yet, but that wasn't stopping them from gaining a reputation. They were quickly establishing an impression about themselves that exists to this day. The general public read about their antics in the newspapers, earning recognition outside of the show-business world, and yet, without the aid of a testimonial dinner, they knew nothing about this group. There was this other side to the club that only members experienced within the confines of their meeting places.

Finding a place to meet was becoming a nuisance because what self-respecting private club has its members meet at a chophouse? They were established, they were incorporated, and they were nomadic. Along with Browne's Chophouse and Keene's Chophouse, they also gathered at the Hotel Hermitage, the Café des Beaux Arts, and the Knickerbocker Theater Building. If you were a member you had better be a daily supporter of the club or you'd wind up in one place while your buddies were spending your dues in another.

That all changed in 1908 when they raised enough money to settle into a place of their own. They held what they referred to as the "first annual event" and pulled out all of the stops—the celebrity Friars performing their bits and strutting their stuff all in the name of a good time and a good cause. Actress Louise Dresser even performed with them, while Victor Herbert led a chorus of the

The Epistle—1917

Friars anthem. The Friars in the audience presumably were mumbling along. The result of their efforts was their very own clubhouse located at 107 West 45th Street. This place had everything: a bar, café, pool table, rooms for lounging, and even one large room for meetings as well as for their testimonial dinners. Members referred to this building as "the friary."

They had a grand time there and discovered that private clubbing had many advantages—eating, drinking, and merriment all came with the territory, and they did it in style. They even had their own newsletter, called *The Epistle*—yet another monastic reference. *The Epistle* reported on happenings around the friary, everything from various events to

Scene *from* The Great Suggestion
By Bertram Marburg and Bennett Musson
As produced by the FRIARS' CLUB FROLIC *of* 1911

lists of members whose mail was returned. *The Epistle* still exists today—only there no longer seems to be an issue with the post office's "return to sender" policy. They had such a blast and enjoyed such tremendous success with the dinners that by 1911 they were ready to move to even bigger and better quarters. Not bad after only three years.

Another event that became as much a part of the Friars as testimonial dinners was the Friars Frolic. While they didn't acknowledge it as such at the time, they deemed their first annual event, after the fact, as being the first Frolic. So when they held a similar event in 1909 it became simply the Friars Frolic. Again, it was a variety format and among the boffo performances was Douglas Fairbanks in a scene from *Nellie the Beautiful Cloak Model* with Louise Dresser. This play was a

Above: *Program cover of the Friars Frolic of 1911 designed by Harrison Fisher*

Top: *A scene from "The Great Suggestion" as performed in the Friars Frolic of 1911. Earle Browne, George M. Cohan, George Evans, Willard D. Coxey, Fred Nible, Tom Lewis, Harry Kelly, Francis X. Hope, John Murray, Julian Eltinge, William Collier, Emmet Corrigan, Samuel Forrest, Raymond Hitchcock, Sam H. Harris*

Opposite: *Irving Berlin on the march in recognition of the Friars Frolic of 1912*

THE FRIARS ON PARADE IN 1912

huge hit at that time and later became a success-ful silent film. It had all of the ingredients of a good melodrama right down to the heroine being tied to the tracks with a train bearing down on her. It's doubtful the train actually chugged into the Frolics rendition, but there is something to be said for going over the top, as the Friars have been wont to do on many occasions. Women were *verboten* at the all-male clubhouse, so Louise must surely have been a welcome sight at their usually stag events.

Since they had such good luck with the first annual event and the second Friars Frolic they added a new twist in 1911—a Friars Frolic on the road. They would travel around the country with their music, jokes, and specialty acts and the money earned would go toward the purchase of a new clubhouse.

For this Frolic Irving Berlin penned a little ditty called "Alexander's Ragtime Band," which became such a huge hit people are still singing it today. After three Frolics, the one in 1911 as well as those in 1912 and 1915, they not only earned enough funds to buy a new building they had enough to build a brand new one from scratch. When they laid the cornerstone on October 21, 1915, George M. Cohan, who was the abbot at the time, broke a sparkling wine bottle over it pro-claiming, "I dedicate this club to art, literature, and good fellowship!"

After one more hugely successful Frolic in

Friars Frolickers of 1916: (Standing) Andrew Mack, Neil O'Brien, James J. Corbett, Harry Kelly, Felix Adler, Harlan Dixon, George Daugherty, Vaughn Comfort, Johnny King, Tom Dingle, Eddie Garvey, Julius Tannen, George Sidney, Tommy Gray, Bert Levy (Sitting) Max Figman, Laddie Cliff, Will Rogers, Sam Harris, Jerry J. Cohan, Louis Mann, Fred Niblo, George M. Cohan, Lew Dockstader, Frank Tinney

1916, the Friars moved into their new digs on 48th Street in Manhattan. It happened on March 22, 1916, amid tons of fanfare. There was a ceremonial march from the old building to the new one. The new clubhouse, which they officially called the monastery, was state-of-the-art, housing a bar, billiard room, grill room, library, gym, wine room, barbershop, forty-two bedrooms with private showers, and a huge banquet hall for all of their entertaining needs. It was an amazing feat for a group who, a mere twelve years earlier, were just griping about a bunch of frauds.

They welcomed in a new era with splashy in-house dinners for the likes of Enrico Caruso, Al Jolson, Calvin Coolidge, Mayor Jimmy Walker, and many other high-profile personalities. These events always managed to get notoriety.

STRUGGLING TO SURVIVE

This building was home to the Friars until 1933, which, as you may surmise, was not the best of years for them. If the Depression wasn't enough to ruin them financially a few slippery hands running the till helped—that and the fact that four club employees sued for back salary. One of those employees listed his job title as bartender, which may not have been the brightest move considering this was during Prohibition and all. The final nail in the coffin was when they were unable to make good on a bill for butter, eggs, and cheese for $1,130.

Friars Club dinner in honor of Enrico Caruso—1916

Above: *Great Hall*

Above: *Architect's rendering of the monastery — 1916–1933*; Below: *Grill Room*   Above: *Billiard Room* Below: *Entrance Hall*

Where's a Friars Frolic when you need one?

But a club does not live by buildings alone, and while the Friars may have lost their monastery, not to mention many members, they never lost their fraternal spirit. The building didn't make the Friar, the camaraderie did, and so they survived—barely—but survive they did. They took rooms in the Hollywood Theatre Building, at the Astor Hotel, at one point even meeting in entertainer Ted Lewis's basement. As Milton Berle, who started hanging out at the Friars when he was just a kid, once said, "We kept moving because it was cheaper than paying rent!"

They finally did settle down a bit on West 47th Street, as Alan King notes: "We went belly up, went broke. Irwin Kramer owned the Edison Hotel, and he was a Friar, and so he gave us two rooms for free—little meeting rooms—and that's how the club stayed afloat."

The officers sent a letter to the members who were able to keep up with the club's drifter lifestyle, just as their turn-of-the-century counterparts had done, saying they were back in business. "Our new quarters consist of the entire tenth floor and the exclusive use of the roof," they wrote, sharing what awaited their fellow Friars. Eventually they could look forward to a rooftop solarium, a handball court, dressing rooms, showers, lockers, and a summer garden. In the meantime, though, they were already set with a card room, lounge, billiard room, and grill. They even noted, "Our landlord will give us complete dining room service at reasonable prices and will also install a bar." It doesn't get any better than that. Well, it did, actually, but for the moment they had a roof over their heads, a place to gather, and bourbon for all.

The dream rooftop solarium may never have come to pass, and the promised amenities may have been slightly exaggerated in the "come back to the fold" letter, but the Friars were still satisfied, despite the cramped quarters. Red Buttons is a Friars Club treasure and holds the distinction of having been a Friar longer than anybody, becoming a member in 1946. "When I joined the Friars Club it was up at the Edison at the annex," he recalls. "It was just a card room, they were struggling. We all helped in those days. There were a bunch of us who were around, who gave of our time and our talents and kept the Friars going."

Buddy Arnold, a TV writer who also produced Friars events, including Frolics and Roasts, remembers this space: "One of the primary things we used to do up in the Edison, we used to watch the fights. A member gave us a sixteen-inch TV set. Do you know how small that is? So we were lucky, and we thought highly of it. There were very few sets in those days, and many a Friar used to stay in that room just to see the Gillette fights on Friday night or the World Series when it came around. Each sporting event that room was jammed with people,

Friar elites Joe E. Lewis, Sophie Tucker, and Al Jolson—circa late 1930s

because most people at home didn't have a set yet in 1945. Then, when Milton came around in '47, millions of sets were sold."

Jean-Pierre Trebot, who is the current executive director of the Friars Club, has heard stories about the boxing interests of the Friars that go back to their first clubhouse. "I'm not sure why, but the Friars have always maintained a connection with the boxing world," he says. "Through the years boxers have appeared on the Friars roster. Champs like James Corbett, Jack Dempsey, Rocky Graziano, and Michael Spinks, for example, have been active members of the club. I know that in the first Friars clubhouse they would hold boxing matches, which may explain why they also had their very own ambulance."

Sports have always been a part of the Friars social life. Granted, for most of these guys, shuffling a deck of cards or racking up billiard balls constitutes strenuous sporting activities, but there have been a few occasions when they actually stepped outside and into the light of day for some fresh air and good wholesome fun. Buddy Arnold remembers: "We once played a baseball game for

ball at all. I think we got one hit in seven innings. But it was for charity."

Richard Lewis can attest to the fact that those involved in sports like to be at the Friars Club. "Bob Costas is a great friend of mine," Lewis says. "Now, here's a man who is obviously a sports kinda guy yet seems to love show-business lore with equal intensity. He's symbolic of the kind of guy who would say to me when he was doing the NBA in New York, 'You're taking me to the Friars today aren't you?' I could have had a motorcycle accident, and he wouldn't say, 'How is your leg?' It's 'What time are we gonna be at the Friars? I think Lasorda's gonna be there too.'

"I mean, that's the first word out of almost everybody's mouth. Once they knew I was a Friar it became like I was a Friar first and a person second. I felt more like a chicken wing than anything else. First of all, it's a great restaurant and the food is amazing. But they had to go there. Particularly if they were in show business, they felt if they weren't seen at the Friars Club, even if they were in the hall of fame, it didn't count yet, it just didn't count yet." For the record, Bob Costas has since joined the club, so he doesn't need Richard to hang out with Lasorda anymore. But he does still need Richard if he wants a few laughs.

The Friars have held dinners and in-house salutes for the likes of George Steinbrenner, Tommy Lasorda, sports columnist Jimmy Cannon, David Cone, and Rod Gilbert. Members who went from the locker room to the dining room have included such superstars as Rusty Staub of the New York Mets, Cal

charity. Milton played, all of the comedians played. Friars against returning war veterans. I think it was 1947 or '48. We faced guys like Phil Weintraub, who was a first baseman for the New York Giants, and Hank Leiber, who was a center fielder. Hank Greenberg was on the Detroit Tigers. I remember they stuck me in the last two innings. We were behind like fourteen nothing, and I came to bat once and a one-legged pitcher name Bert Shepard of the Washington Senators struck me out on three pitches. I swung when the catcher was throwing the ball back at him. I couldn't see the

Ramsey of the Knicks, and basketball greats Willis Reed and Walt Frazier, among others. Baseball legend Joe DiMaggio holds a special place. As if his Hall of Fame status isn't enough he also has that Marilyn Monroe connection that bumps him into his own showbiz category. The list of sports personalities who have attended events or hung out at the monastery is as endless as the number of comedians. This is a testament, perhaps, to the fact that people who sweat for a living love to laugh.

BERLE TO THE RESCUE

Just as George M. Cohan helped the Friars into their building in 1916 with Frolics and fundrais-

ers, Milton Berle met the challenge during his rein as abbot from 1940 to 1945. (For the record, he held the position again from 1947 to 1953 and once more in 1956.) He worked his tail off promoting the club to fill the ranks. Alan King, a fellow abbot, says: "I would have to say that literally, single-handedly, Milton brought the club back. He was big in New York. This was before television, and then of course when he became Mr. Television he really gave the club a huge boost. A lot of these giants, these icons, they really took the club seriously. This was really very fraternal."

Buddy Arnold also gives Berle the thumbs up in the dedication department: "In '48 Berle became

Friars Club ambulance ready for action after a Friars boxing match — circa 1930s

the biggest thing in the United States for comedy when he started his *Texaco Star Theater* show. He was tremendous. So due to the fact of his being the abbot of the club it started to get members. They came in droves."

America has its bald eagle, and the Friars Club has its Milton Berle—bold symbols of strength and independence. He once said, "I gave my life for the Friars!" And he meant it. Berle may not have started the Friars Club, but he clearly is the man responsible for keeping the fraternal dream alive. Comedian Freddie Roman, the current dean, says of the man who would be king of the Friars, "He was a driving force in this club before he went to LA, and was responsible in many ways for the continuance of the club. When he came east he would come here everyday for lunch or for dinner. He sat in that corner and commanded the room. Everybody was in awe of the fact that he was here."

Buddy Arnold recalls a Berle Friarly moment outside of the monastery: "On Sunday nights, after the last show in the nightclubs, all the comedians in town, plus every guy from the Friars, would come over to Leon and Eddie's, that was the comedians night out. They used to do shows from like midnight to three in the morning and Milton was always the emcee. He represented the Friars and every comic in the Friars was on the bill.

"One night, Youngman was there. He usually got on early—early was like one in the morning. Two o'clock came, three o'clock came, and Youngman hadn't been on yet. Milton is ready to close up shop. He was kidding Youngman by keeping him off. In comes Youngman in disgust and angry, leading into Leon and Eddie's a patrolman on a horse. In those days they used to patrol the streets on horseback, so Youngman went out and got the cop who was patrolling 53rd St. He led

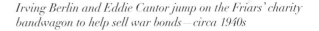
Irving Berlin and Eddie Cantor jump on the Friars' charity bandwagon to help sell war bonds – circa 1940s

him right through the door, on to the stage. The cop on the horse grabbed Milton by his neck, lifted him up on the horse, and walked out with him. Henny took the stage and said, 'That will teach him to keep me to last.'"

Comedian Jeffrey Ross recalls those times Berle was in town: "I loved when Uncle Miltie would stop by. Everything would stop. He made the staff nervous. After all, he *was* the Friars Club. Legend has it that the building was once his home. He probably needed the whole fourth floor for his penis." Well he's half right—the building wasn't his home. But oh, the mileage that legendary penis got at Roasts and various events throughout Berle's

Harry Delf and Milton Berle lead the celebration of the Friars first anniversary in their 55th St. monastery — 1958

ing to get back on its feet in the mid-forties. Delf, a vaudevillian who became a successful film executive, had been a Friar since the days when George M. Cohan was hoofing around the halls. He convinced Berle to become the abbot to help things along. According to Harry Delf Jr.: "After the Second World War there were like sixty or seventy members, and my father decided that it was a shame and that they should really start to expand the club. They didn't have any money; they didn't have anything. He got the money by coming up with the idea of reinstituting these dinners, these Roasts."

reign. Its size was the premise of some of the funniest and filthiest jokes in Friar history.

"Everyone was their own pope at the Friars Club, it seemed to me," says Richard Lewis. "It seemed like if Milton was there, I can't think of anyone else who could upstage that. I mean, I once got down on my knees and I kissed his hand and Milton got upset. I said, 'What's wrong?' and he said, 'Kiss the ring.' Just the hand wasn't enough, and of course I screamed 'cause it was just too funny."

Harry Delf was the dean when the club was try-

Berle and Delf must have done something right because in 1949 the Friars purchased a two-story brick garage and dance studio located on West 56th Street and after renovating it moved in on May 12, 1950. There wasn't an inch of empty space to be found around the club's semi-circular bar on the first floor once all the Friars trooped in to toast the end of their lean years with champagne. They paid off their mortgage, in full, a year and a half later. The Friars were back on their feet and open for business!

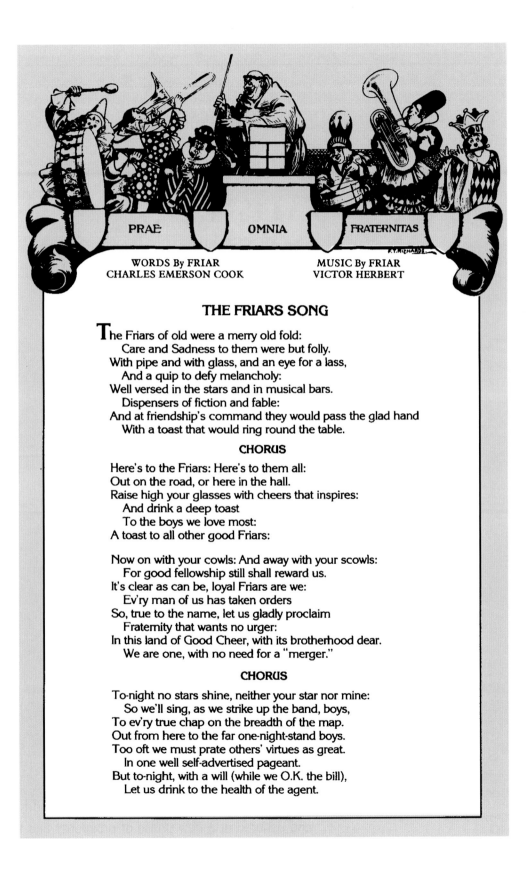

PRAE OMNIA FRATERNITAS

WORDS By FRIAR
CHARLES EMERSON COOK

MUSIC By FRIAR
VICTOR HERBERT

THE FRIARS SONG

The Friars of old were a merry old fold:
  Care and Sadness to them were but folly.
With pipe and with glass, and an eye for a lass,
  And a quip to defy melancholy:
Well versed in the stars and in musical bars.
  Dispensers of fiction and fable:
And at friendship's command they would pass the glad hand
  With a toast that would ring round the table.

CHORUS

Here's to the Friars: Here's to them all:
Out on the road, or here in the hall.
Raise high your glasses with cheers that inspires:
  And drink a deep toast
  To the boys we love most:
A toast to all other good Friars:

Now on with your cowls: And away with your scowls:
  For good fellowship still shall reward us.
It's clear as can be, loyal Friars are we:
  Ev'ry man of us has taken orders
So, true to the name, let us gladly proclaim
  Fraternity that wants no urger:
In this land of Good Cheer, with its brotherhood dear.
  We are one, with no need for a "merger."

CHORUS

To-night no stars shine, neither your star nor mine:
  So we'll sing, as we strike up the band, boys,
To ev'ry true chap on the breadth of the map.
Out from here to the far one-night-stand boys.
Too oft we must prate others' virtues as great.
  In one well self-advertised pageant.
But to-night, with a will (while we O.K. the bill),
  Let us drink to the health of the agent.

performers eking out a humble living. "These people didn't have money," says Friars Club Maitre d' Frank Capitelli, who started with the club as a waiter in 1960. "One thing I remember, a liverwurst sandwich in those days cost forty-five cents. They used to come over, they'd have a bowl of soup, they'd eat a dozen rolls, then they'd say, 'Oh, I'm not hungry.' They couldn't afford it.

"They survived their own way. It's not so sophisticated like today. In those days they were simple good people. A few were smart to save their money but not like today. In those days it didn't exist. You take a guy like Joe E. Lewis, who reached a point that he was broke completely until he had someone manage his money. He used to come over to the club and take care of a lot of guys who couldn't afford things. A lot of comedians couldn't afford a meal. Milton Berle was the same way. They used to take care of everybody. They gave away money. They used to love to do that. It was a way of living in those days." Frank Sinatra was also philanthropic with destitute performers, but he was extremely private it about.

Charity among the Friars is all well and good but it won't pay that butter, eggs, and cheese bill. Let's face it, prices have risen a lot since 1933, so rather than losing yet another building, something needed to be done to help things along. According to Harry Delf, Jr.: "When my father was a member early on, there were no non-theatrical people and it became another big scene in the club as to whether or not they wanted to take non-professionals. I would guess he would say we have got to take in non-professionals, but we have to limit it." Which is exactly what they did.

"It started out as a theatrical club," Milton Berle recalled later, "then one day I walked in there and got measured for a suit. Joke. Meaning that we had a lot of laymen because that's the way we started to get more members that were not show business members." Not to mention non-pros, as they are technically known on their applications, bring with them a built-in audience for the performers who love an audience, even during lunch.

"Jessel used to call the civilians, the non-show people, 'furriers,'" remembers Alan King. "We took the non-pros in because we were broke and a lot of the civilians wanted to be around show people. That kept the club going."

Jack L. Green is the dean emeritus of the Friars and remembers earlier times: "The feel of the club was really a theatrical feel. I'd walk into the building and I knew almost everybody in the dining room. They were agents, they were managers, they were performers, they were music publishers, songwriters, musicians. It was a camaraderie. Everybody knew everybody. Whatever we discussed, there was an affinity about what we were discussing. When they allowed non-pros in they charged them a lot more money for the privilege of being around people in the entertainment business. And there was a waiting list and that waiting list went on for years. But it is true how it changed. I remember sitting in the bar upstairs one day and somebody in the corner was showing swatches of material, and it was very different than somebody downstairs swapping jokes. The commodity changed."

Of course, this new shift in membership did make for an interesting mix around the clubhouse, as Jean-Pierre Trebot observes: "The dichotomy of the Friars is such that you have a wide spectrum of income. You have young performers barely eking out a living, and you have superstars making super salaries. And now add to the roster corporate tycoons with golden parachutes."

Red Buttons admits times changed but concurs about the need to diversify: "In '46, when I joined, it was almost 100 percent show business. Not today for a very, very good reason—the doors wouldn't be open if it was a 100 percent show business. Money talks. It's the name of the game, and that's what has happened. You walk up there and you look around and you see business people."

THE LADIES ARRIVE

If the thought of having non-pros join the club was alarming, you can imagine the temperature of the room whenever discussion of allowing women into the club came up. "When it started in the early years," says Buttons, "it was just a place for the guys to get away, have a cognac, smoke a cigar, and if they wanted to talk dirty, they could do it. Because in those days, it was not the fashionable thing to do. You couldn't say 'hell' or 'damn' in front of women. You wouldn't. It was off limits."

They threw this discussion around for decades on whether or not to make the ladies members, but in spite of their no-women ban they did honor them at dinners and an occasional Roast through the years. Nellie Revell was the first woman to be honored. In 1924 the reporter and vaudeville publicist was given a formal testimonial dinner at the Hotel Astor. Sophie Tucker held a very special place among the Friars. When she was roasted in 1953 Frank Sinatra sang that she was "The only Friar without balls." Sophie was also one of the very few women actually allowed to hang around the monastery. "She shaved! She was a rough son of a bitch," laughs Alan King when Sophie's name comes up. "She cursed like a stevedore. Martha Raye would also come in and, oh what a mouth she had, so we didn't consider them women."

NO FEMALE MEMBERS 57

Friars Club

"THAT'S a lady ?!"

© Printed with permission from Paul Rigby and the *New York Post*

Paul Rigby, former cartoonist for the New York Post, *drew his vision of the Friars letting women into the monastery—1988*

Carol Burnett with her dinner journal before she got hit with a pie — 1973

As Harry Delf, Jr. recalls: "My father wanted to have women in the club but not a whole lot of women. He sort of inspired that movement but on a restrained level. I remember the kitchen was the main problem for the club. It never made any money. He used to tell me no kitchen ever makes any money in a private club. So he always used to try to come up with approaches. I think that's when they decided to have women come in, because most guys didn't want to show up for a special dinner unless they could bring their wives or their girlfriends."

So it was decided that women could come to the club but on a limited basis as guests only, and they were never allowed above the second floor. "It was a men's club only until five o'clock, really," says Freddie Roman. "So if you were not here at lunchtime, if you were, for example, a member who would use the club in the evenings, it really wasn't that different. Women were permitted in the club-house and wives or significant others, or whatever, so there were always women around in the evenings. But in the afternoons it was a bastion of testosterone, there's no question about it. I remember Berle one day sitting in the corner table and stood up at his table and told the filthiest joke. Just stood up and people loved the fact that he would do it. But, of course, that doesn't happen anymore."

Jack L. Green recalls a snag or two with the women's policy at the Friars: "They weren't allowed above the second floor and they weren't allowed in the building until like four or five o'clock. I remem-

Dinah Shore, Barbra Streisand, Carol Burnett, and Elizabeth Taylor were all toasted during this pre-women-as-members era, while Martha Raye, Lucille Ball, Totie Fields, and Phyllis Diller suffered the same slings and arrows the guys endured at their Roasts. So it was only a matter of time before the women would also enjoy the same camaraderie in the monastery as their male counterparts.

ber, I had a meeting with Shirley MacLaine there, and it was a three-o'clock meeting, and I wasn't quite sure so I said, 'Make it 4:30,' and we had the meeting on the second floor."

Allowing women into the building was hardly a solution to the issue of female membership. "It became a problem," says Green. "We had a member of the board at that time who did a lot of work with CBS, and because of the fact that we didn't allow women in he resigned from the board. I don't know if it was pressure from CBS or he felt he had to do it because of his business association with CBS. But there was a lot of pressure all around on it. The women came in under my administration. We held a bunch of meetings prior to that, getting everybody's idea on bringing women in.

"What a lot of the members didn't realize is that it took us about two years in planning before we even broached the subject. We had to figure out planning locker rooms and other facilities for the women so it could be an equality once they did come in. When we had that straight in our minds, then we took it to the membership for a vote. A lot of the members were apprehensive, but it's been very healthy. I find that the women are very active in the club on committees and on everything, and they participate, and it gives a nice feeling around the building."

In 1988 the Friars allowed women to join the club as members, much to the chagrin of many. "A lot of the old timers were crazed to see a woman at lunch here at the club," recalls Freddie Roman. "But they got over it. We never had anyone quit because of it. Which was good. It just has evolved into our way of life and wonderfully so."

Alan King remembers one member who wasn't particularly thrilled. "Henny Youngman was the biggest opponent," King says. "He was so against

it he threatened to quit the club." Lucky for the Friars he never carried that out.

Longtime Friar Jerry Stiller, always the gentleman, had mixed feelings about women in the club but not for reasons of preserving the all-male bastion. "I was afraid they were going to hear things they shouldn't hear," Stiller explains. "I said to myself, '*Shonder shonder*!' But then I remembered we saw Belle Barth at Caesars Palace and God she was funny. This woman who seemed like a kind of sweet grandmother-type, but oh my God she'd let out these words. I said to myself, 'She comes from a place of women who can make you laugh, and I don't care what words they use they have a right to do it.' That's what it was all about so why not allow women to come in? And here I was working with my wife, what would I say? 'Anne, you can't come to the Friars.' You can't put it into gender when it comes to comedy. Comedy is when something is funny, it's funny. It was a great moment, I think, that the Friars were willing to take that step."

For Frank Capitelli there was a special moment that said it all about finally opening up the entire monastery to women after eighty-four years. "There was this young girl, she was about twenty-two years old, and she was the daughter of a member," he remembers. "She used to be here a lot for dinner but in those days no woman was allowed to go above the second floor. No lady ever put a foot above the second floor until 1988. Just the girls that used to work in the office, they used to go upstairs, that's it. But they never got out of the elevator. The night that we allowed ladies in they opened up every room for everybody to see the building.

"So this girl comes over to me, and says, 'Frank, I'm so excited to go upstairs to the third floor. I've been coming here ever since I was little

Liza Minnelli performing at the Friars Foundation dinner in honor of Warner Music exec Frank Military — 1995

girl, but I never was allowed to go above the second floor and tonight I'm going above the second floor.' She was all excited. She came up, she went to the fourth floor, fifth floor, she almost was crying. I said, 'What happened to you?' She said, 'I felt so disappointed. I don't know what I was expecting. Some kind of fantasy. All this time I had a fantasy about something that was forbidden.'"

Something that was forbidden—so aptly put when talking about the Friars Club!

Liza Minnelli is the Friars' first official female member and has mentioned how pleased she is to be a Friar on more than one occasion. Joan Rivers

was also among the first women recruited to fill the female ranks. "They were bringing women in and I was in the first group they asked to join," Rivers says. "It was Liza Minnelli and a few more of us, and we were the first ones in. I said, 'Of course, whatever you want, it's a wonderful organization.' It was wonderful they picked me. I thought that was very special."

With change comes firsts, and the Friars' first woman to serve on the board of governors was Frances Preston, the president of BMI. The club's constitution states that Friars are not eligible to run for the board until they have been a member

Below: They've come a long way baby! Ann Reinking, Judy Collins, and Tyne Daly strut their stuff for the Friars camera at the in-house salute to Judy Collins—1995

Above: *Susie Essman, Judy Gold, Joy Behar, and Brett Butler at the Friars Roast of Rob Reiner—2000*

for five years, so in October of 1993 Ms. Preston made her governing debut. Not only was she an active member of the board, she is also the recipient of the Friars Foundation's Applause Award. Let's face it, those press agents of yore are turning in their graves over the progress women have made, so to Frances, more power to ya!

Sally Jessy Raphael is a ranking officer in a club that less than twenty years ago barely allowed her in the building. "Once you've opened the barn door, what do you do?" says Raphael. She currently is third in command as prior of the club and has never felt her sex affected how the male Friars treated her. "I've never known that," she says. "I joke about it but there's no feeling, and you can do whatever you want. Women have been nothing but a tremendous help to this club. Women who get into this club really work for it. Mae West should have been a member."

Susie Essman says being a woman at the Friars can be physically draining: "They love to touch. It's all they can do at this point, so they hold your hand, and with the other hand they'll stroke the top of your hand. It's like a Purell moment every time I walk into the Friars Club. You have to Purell the minute you leave there. There's so much touching."

Of course, an artist is going to recognize a thing of beauty, and LeRoy Neiman is no exception. "It's nice having women around," he says. "Also, you see not just pretty young girls but you see women, mature women, intelligent women, funny women. They're not just there. They're part of it. They improve the ambiance."

The Friars may still have some work ahead of them though to get the women to utilize the amenities more if you listen to Joy Behar's response when asked if she uses the gym: "No. No. Is anyone there?" One or two maybe but either the female Friars are in much better shape than the men or they just don't want to bother climbing over any napping Friars to get to the treadmill.

"I gotta say though, you look at it, it *looks* like a boys club with the pool room and the barbershop but I don't feel that," says Judy Gold. "I feel like there's Joy, there's Susie, there's a bunch of the big mouths, and we can hold our own. I don't think that they think we're any less funny. I think about it now, I can't even imagine that place without the women."

ON TO THE FUTURE

While there is an image of ribaldry to uphold, the Friars Club does have, and always has had, a benevolent side. Throughout their century-long reign in entertainment they have been there for those in need. Whether it be hosting a Thanksgiving dinner at the monastery during WWI for soldiers on leave or making the holidays brighter for underprivileged children, they maintain a valuable presence in the community.

The Friars Foundation was created in 1977, and under the aegis of the current administrators—Chairman Leo Greenland and President Cy Leslie—the foundation's mission is to foster the performing arts. They accomplish this through the Friars Foundation Performing Arts Scholarship Program as well as by providing grants to not-for-profit performing arts groups and general charities. Their major fund-raising event is an annual dinner at which they honor individuals in the industry for their humanitarian and charitable endeavors. At the dinner the honorees receive the Friars Foundation's Lifetime Achievement Applause Award. They also present the Creative Achievement Award at this event to a celebrity who has given his or her time and is highly regarded for charitable giving.

The ever-evolving Friars Club has not lasted a hundred years just because its members tell the best dirty jokes, though there is something to be said for that, in spite of the Vatican having had a longer run, so to speak. The club has always had an odd reputation. On the one hand, it is one of the most progressive of organizations. Let's face it: they are the ones who created an event solely for the purpose of, pardon the French, "ripping guests of honors a new asshole." If that's not considered liberal and topical, then what is? Yet, on the other hand, the biggest joke among Friar comedians is, "What is the average age of the Friars? Deceased!" Yeah, yeah, it's funny, and sometimes, depending on the decade, there might even be a hint of truth, but the Friars are here to stay in spite of the punch lines.

The club does need to think about future generations carrying on the legacy, but so far that has gone off without a hitch. There has to be something to this Friars Club thing if it has survived the passing of George M. Cohan just as it survived the passing of Milton Berle. Granted, a concerted effort is needed to push things along a bit, but hey, you're reading a book celebrating their centennial so they must be doing something right. Besides, if they survived the milkman's dunning notice and the faux bartender's unemployment woes, not to mention the Depression and a transition of the entertainment industry from the east to the west, they can certainly handle the new millennium.

Maybe the hobbits can help them on their journey, seeing as New Line Cinema executives Robert Shaye and Michael Lynne, the producers of *The Lord of the Rings* films, are Friars. As Jean-Pierre Trebot notes, "Captains of the entertainment industry have always felt comfortable at the Friars.

In the past you would find William Paley, founder of CBS, Robert Sarnoff of NBC, Milton Rackmil of Universal, Leo Jaffe from Columbia Pictures, Lew Wasserman of Universal Pictures, Bernard Myerson of Loews Theaters, so many of the powerhouses in show business find their way here."

This is an interesting time to witness the people sitting in the dining room. There's David Brown, the prolific producer of many films including *A Few Good Men*, and at another table might be Eli Roth, who recently directed the critically acclaimed thriller *Cabin Fever*. It's an interesting mix of various generations of successful moviemakers all chowing down on kasha varnishkas.

Richard Lewis keeps his angst in check while making the Friars laugh in the Milton Berle Room — 1990s

The monastery spread on the next two pages reflects how the interior of the building looked when home to Martin Erdmann from 1909 to 1937
Far left: The current Friars monastery (how it looked when the Friars first moved into it in 1957). Now, in place of the bookshop to the left, is a Duane Reade; and to the right is a huge skyscraper known as the Park Avenue Tower. What a difference a few decades makes
Top left: Martin Erdmann's dining room on the second floor had elegance and grace. The Friars Celebrity Room Bar that is there today still retains the very same elements
Left bottom: First floor of Martin Erdmann's home looking into what is now the Friars Billy Crystal Bar
Center top: This was a living room in Martin Erdmann's house that is now the Friars Milton Berle Room where Mr. Erdmann would surely find a little too much living going on
Center bottom: This charming sitting room on the third floor is still quite charming as the Friars Ed Sullivan Room, which houses the Bernie and Muriel Myerson Library — an audio/visual library for members
Right top: This third-floor room was possibly a bedroom in Martin Erdmann's time, but today it is known as the William B. Williams Billiard Room where there is no sleeping allowed
Right bottom: Martin Erdmann's first-floor study. Today the only studying that goes on is how to make the perfect martini as it is the Friars Billy Crystal Bar

Comedian Stewie Stone, who has held the office of scribe as well as chairman of the Friars Entertainment Committee, may not have been a young pup when he joined the club, but he was certainly in tune to a younger way of thinking. "It's a funny thing. I'm an older guy but I had that young feel," he says. "I was a hip guy and I thought, 'Oh the Friars isn't for me.' And all the older guys said, 'Why don't you join?' And one day they talked me into it. I said, 'Okay, I'll join.' I was around New York more and when I joined, I realized how great it was. When you look at it from the outside, sometimes as a comedian, you say, 'Oh the older guys are here, the Berle's and this and I'm with the younger guys.' You don't realize how terrific it is and what a fellowship it is. That's the mentality that goes on today. Before you join it you don't realize what a great fraternity it is and how much you learn."

There was a time when Jeffrey Ross was the youngest Friar. He was one of the young comics who not only epitomized the MTV/Comedy Central generation but also quickly mastered the art of the Roasts. It got so that when he was introduced at events outside of the Friars Club they would include his being the hit of the Roasts. "When I first started doing the Roasts, I was also very involved in the alternative comedy scene downtown," says Ross. "Those comics would always goof on me for being part of the stuffy Friars tradition. Eventually, I got all those downtown comics to start showing up at Friars events. That was very gratifying. I even got a special award for being a 'Membership Maven.'"

Lest anyone question the stuffiness of the Friars, Ross, who has had hit specials on the young-demographic-grabbing Comedy Central, went from telling jokes at Roasts to dictating policy at board-of-governors meetings. He was elected to the board when his five years kicked in and regards the Friars as more than a mausoleum. "I think of the Friars as a living museum of showbiz," he explains. "It's a place where beginners and legends can learn from each other. I once moderated a 'comics only' seminar in which Buddy Hackett answered a roomful of younger comics' questions. That day, I think, Buddy learned as much as we did."

In order for this funny torch to be passed there needs to be individuals who carry with them some morsel of the previous generation. Richard Lewis possesses such a quality. "Red Buttons said that I reminded him of the kind of comedians that they used to be but for my generation. That always meant a lot to me, and it came from a lot of them in different ways. I know what they meant. They meant that I would be up there pounding it out like I was in the Borsht Belt, but I would be doing it for my generation—I was an extension. One day I did a show in New York, and I got a great review and Stephen Holden in the *New York Times* said that he considered me the transitional link between those comedians and the new generation. When I read that I felt like a million bucks and then I really felt like a Friar."

"Every generation of Friars has experienced the need to rejuvenate," admits Jean-Pierre Trebot. "We are at that point again in the Friars timeline where new blood will see us well into the new millennium. We're lucky. We have a history that we can bank on. I laugh when I sit in board meetings and older Friars say, 'We need to update the pictures on the walls, get rid of Benny and Burns and Al Jolson, let's get younger faces up there.' Afterward some young Friar on the board will inevitably come up to me and say, 'You know, those old faces are the reason I'm here. It's those old show-business legends whose foot-

Rob Reiner helps punch up Billy Crystal's jokes during the Friars Roast of Rob Reiner—2000

Anne Meara living any woman's dream—roasting her husband on national television at the Friars Comedy Central Roast of Jerry Stiller—1999

steps I'm proud to walk in.' Which is really quite refreshing to hear."

In recent years the movers and shakers of the current entertainment era have visited the monastery or joined. Not so long ago a group of writers from *Seinfeld* stopped by to soak up some local color and the result was an episode about Jerry trying to join the Friars Club. Writers for David Letterman's and Conan O'Brian's late-night shows have joined, and *Saturday Night Live* comics and writers have always found a fun—and yes, trendy—time at the monastery.

The Friars name is certainly out there. The

1955 film *Seven Little Foys* showcased Bob Hope sharing a song and dance scene with Jimmy Cagney's George M. Cohan. Both hoofers danced at the film version of Cohan's Friars Club dinner. Neil Simon's 1975 *The Sunshine Boys*, the semi-fictional account of the rocky comeback of Smith and Dale, which earned George Burns an Academy Award, filmed a scene at the monastery. This is the only movie to bear that distinction. The film's co-stars, Burns and Walter Matthau, were both feted with a dinner by the Friars and an elderly Joe Smith was in attendance.

When Billy Crystal filmed *Mr. Saturday Night* his character was based on a composite of several Friars, and it also has a scene that takes place in the Friars Club. *Let Me In, I Hear Laughter* is a documentary about the Friars Club. Written, produced, and directed by twenty-something filmmaker Dean Ward, it aired on Cinemax, garnering excellent reviews. Good Lord, even Homer Simpson was roasted by the Springfield Friars Club! Krusty the

Ben Stiller and Janeane Garofalo at his dad, Jerry Stiller's Roast — 1999

Clown is welcome to be roastmaster at a Friars Roast anytime. So, say what you will about the Friars being full of drooling, old has-beens—okay, that would not be a total lie—but the bottom line is that this private club caters to people of all ages—and *that* is what makes it so wonderful.

In 1998 the Friars found themselves catering to a new demographic altogether when they began televising their Roasts on Comedy Central. Suddenly it was the 18-34 year-olds who were not only hearing about the Friars Club for the first time, but they were laughing their asses off in the process. The Friars produced five annual Roasts in conjunction with Comedy Central—Drew Carey, Jerry Stiller, Rob Reiner, Hugh Hefner, and Chevy Chase, and it added a new word in the Friars lexicon—ratings.

Rob Reiner experienced a Comedy Central Roast in 2000. Millions of viewers watched his ego deflate before their eyes—you've already read a sampling of one of the jokes from Alan King, and

there were plenty more where that one came from. Before the cameras rolled, Rob hoped for the best. "Just that they not make any jokes about my penis, that's the only thing I require," he said. "No penis jokes." Poor Rob. He was so wrong.

But television did add a new dimension to the honor, and there was cause for concern, as Reiner expressed prior to the event: "I remember those old Dean Martin Roasts that George Schlatter used to produce. I just hope that they don't cut to me and I'm pretending to laugh. I hope it's actually funny so I'm actually laughing instead of faking laughing like they used to do with those shows. Everything was hysterically funny. Everything at the same level of funniness. Of course, that was George Schlatter with a machine too. They don't use a machine for this, do they?

"The fact that it's on television will make it tamer than it otherwise would be. They can't get too brutal with me, right? They'll just do it in a non-dirty way.... I have to have my head examined!"

The Comedy Central Roasts opened up a new era of recognition for the Friars, not to mention those who were brave enough to endure the ribbing nationwide. For Jerry Stiller it was a bit of a shock. "I can't tell you, from the day that thing was shown, people would come up to me on the street—young people mostly, people in their twenties up to their forties—everyone saying, 'We thought that was the funniest show we ever saw.' That was the big payoff for it. I kept saying, 'What did I do?' I guess you could say it was the way I squirmed. I was overwhelmed by the response."

Where do they go from here? For the Friars there is only one way they know and that is up. "My gut feeling is that with the new younger members of the club who really, genuinely love it," says Freddie Roman, "the club will continue for a long, long time. There's enough show people in the New York area that care and every year we get more and more—we definitely have a future here."

For the Friars, when you speak of moving forward you can't help but consider the legacy that has been handed down. It is a gift, as Norm Crosby notes: "There is so much history here and that's part of tradition. But it's awesome. You can't come into the club and not think, wow, maybe George Burns sat here. Maybe Jack

Margaret Cho and Drew Carey get cutesy for the camera at Drew's Friars Club Roast — 1998

Benny sat here. They walked on this carpet where I have my feet now. Maybe they stood there? It's an accomplishment to be a member of this club. An achievement that every member should be aware of and be proud of and be happy with. That you were accepted. You wear your Friars pin with such dignity because this means something. People look at you and say, 'What is that?' 'Oh, well, I'm a Friar.' 'Oh, really?'"

Who is to say where the Friars will end up and if their bicentennial book will be as much fun as this one, but they certainly are a resilient bunch. They've come a long way from that group of eleven press agents and along the way have gathered a reputation that is unique to show business. Jerry Stiller pretty much sums up the need for a place called the Friars Club: "I love to watch other comedians—I go crazy. I laugh at straight lines. I am one of those people who have a desperate need to laugh. Some people will say, 'Oh, he's not funny or she's not funny,' and I say, 'Yes they are.' I can see the humor in almost anybody who breaks his or her neck to get up there and try. So I see this idea of what the Friars do. It's keeping the baby alive, it's keeping that child within us alive, and it's very necessary and no one else would do this."

CHAPTER THREE

MAKE 'EM LAUGH, CRY, AND BEG FOR MORE

Events in the Early Years

Opposite page: *Program cover for Friars Club dinner in honor of George M. Cohan — 1910*

Throughout its history, the one constant within the Friars Club has been entertainment. Laughter is the Friars' natural resource and has enriched the legacy that has been handed down through a century of testimonial dinners, Friars Frolics, and celebrity Roasts.

"It started with George M. Cohan," says Alan King. "They used to have these nights—the Players Club called them Pipe Nights—and so when these guys came over to the Friars Club they used to hold similar black-tie dinners. They didn't have a dais per se but very big tables, and they used to sit around them. Mayor Jimmy Walker, the Schuberts, and everybody would get up and say just about anything. It was all men; it didn't matter. And these were very funny guys. Very witty." Not to mention their humor was also very biting,

according to most accounts of these early events.

COHAN AND JOLSON

The Friars honored George M. Cohan in 1910, and this evening apparently broke all attendance records—or, one assumes, whatever attendance figures they had logged during their six years in operation. The crème de la crème of New York's entertainment, social, and political elite filed into the Astor Hotel ballroom to pay tribute to the man who was the toast of Broadway. One of the speakers was A. L. Erlanger, who was named for Abraham Lincoln but whose reputation would never secure him a national holiday. Several sources have labeled this successful theater owner and producer one of the most hated men in twentieth-century show business. He made and destroyed careers with impunity. How nice for George to have such a guy there to give testimony to his success.

Then again, why wouldn't the Friars, who were quickly gaining a reputation for roasting instead of toasting, want such a speaker to stir things up a bit? Much to the chagrin of many Friars, Erlanger turned in quite a "toast" with nothing but kind things to say. He suggested the audience condemn Cohan for the crime of "possessing super skills in everything he undertakes." And ended with his own version of Cohan's famous exit line, "My mother thanks you, my father thanks you, my wife thanks you, my sister thanks you, my baby thanks you, and I thank you." What fun is that?

Cohan was so shocked at the accolades that he was stricken with stage fright, probably for the first time in his life. He was unable to utter a word of his speech. But he rallied with the following: "The managers tell me I'm a good actor, and the actors say I'm a bully manager. The musicians tell me I ought to write nothing but plays, and the playwrights tell me I should confine myself exclusively to music. Why, no man could help getting along with so many people saying these encouraging things to him. One critic out in Seattle wrote about me that he had been informed that I could write a play in twenty-four hours and that after seeing *The Yankee Prince* he had no reason to believe otherwise."

Bombastic as ever, though, Cohan closed with: "I have only one request to make for you tonight and that is, wherever you are, whether it be Lynn, Massachusetts, or in the wilds of Africa, that you please mention my name as much as possible." Let's hope George M. is happy knowing that this book is still carrying out that request.

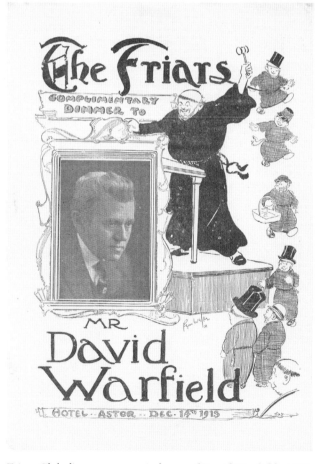

Friars Club dinner program in honor of David Warfield—1913

Another noteworthy entertainment milestone happened this evening. Colonel William F. Cody, also known as "Buffalo Bill," was a speaker, and after paying homage to George, he announced his retirement from show business. These Friars events will do that to you—make you want to get out of the business. But you do exit laughing, so how bad can that be?

For some Friars, these private events offer opportunities not afforded in more orthodox venues. As David Hyde Pierce, who was the roastmaster for Kelsey Grammer's 1996 Roast, notes, "The fun of that and the freedom of the Friars Club is that it's a private event for those people. Just like there are things I might say to a friend in private that I wouldn't say to them in a public place over a micro-

Ryan Walker cartoon that appeared inside the dinner journal for the George M. Cohan dinner—1910

Far left: *Boys will be girls at the Friars Frolic at Lou Walters's Latin Quarter — 1951*
Above: *The shenanigans at the same Friars Frolic — 1951*
Left: *Friars Frolic program — 1958*

Above left: *Jimmy Johnston, Pat Boone, and Jack Barry at the Friars Frolic — 1958* Above right: *Red Buttons and Dagmar at the Friars Frolic — 1958*

Delf and William Frawley. But even so, to be able to see Delf, a Friars Club rock, and Frawley, Fred Mertz from *I Love Lucy*, in action would have been a gem for the archives.

Cohan did, however, show up at a Frolic in 1931, and he brought on stage his son Georgie, a student at Georgetown University, to hoof alongside him. It was the first time the father-and-son team danced together professionally. Mayor Jimmy Walker, who received several salutes from the Friars, was in the audience. He stood up and said he was happy to have lived to see in action the third generation of the greatest of theatrical families.

This Frolic also featured what must have been yet another amazing moment, as noted by *Variety*: "Cohan introduced the composers in the pianolog interlude, one of the show's most notable presentations. The Friars' leader said that the club had brought together the first 'piano bugs' twenty-one years ago, the innovation then making the frolics famous. Irving Berlin, George Gershwin, Walter Donaldson, Milton Ager, Gus Edwards, Harry Warren, and Harry Ruby were at the grands."

Despite the Friars' roaming phase, whether they hung their cowls in the Hollywood Theatre Building, Astor Hotel, or Edison Hotel, they still maintained their reputation in entertainment as the party boys who never found a joke or a song they couldn't turn into a full-fledged production. Buddy Arnold was part of the new generation of Friars in the '40s. "I recall once, Milton—who I had just gotten to know, I wrote some stuff for him—he went to the Latin Quarter one night, where a couple of the Friars got up and said a few words. They told them about the club having re-opened," Arnold says.

"The first event I can remember as a Friar, Milton wanted to do what they called the Friars Frolic," Arnold continues. "They'd rented a hotel room, much like the affairs are now. I don't think it was formal, though. And a bunch of stars came on and they plugged the Friars mainly. I don't know whether the money was given for charity then, I'm not sure. The charity would have been the Friars. They needed it."

The ever-evolving club discovered that the Frolic was a sure way to showcase the Friars' talents and raise much-needed funds. According to Buddy Arnold, "Almost every Friar of the fifty or sixty members was in the show doing something, even as an extra. I joined in 1947 and I was head of the entertainment committee there from 1948, I'd say, all the way until I left to live in California in 1971. It was a hell of a run. And the kind of shows we did, I remember, we had sketches now and then. See, it wasn't all entertainers like singers and comedians standing and talking. We put on an occasional sketch, like the Directors Guild would do for their show.

"The backbone of it, of course, was the entertainment by the stars. Let's say we were honoring someone like Jack Benny. I took a few well-known people, I dressed them up in Friars robes, and they'd open each one of these big annual shows we did. They would open up wearing the costume of a Friar and singing special lyrics about the guest of honor who we were honoring. I'd put together comedy lyrics to about twelve different songs that were appropriate for these, about the guest of honor and his life, what he did. So, the shows were a little different then. But we used to work on them all year 'round. There was no clubhouse yet."

THE ROAST

When things get to be one hundred years old, be it a country, a monument, a person—God bless them—or a private entertainment club, somewhere along the way the record-keeping is going to run into a few snags. Files get misplaced, artifacts damaged, or historical data just plain forgotten. All are true for the Friars. They also lost a year or two—or seven—when they wandered around the desert of Manhattan following their own version of Moses for that long-awaited homeland.

One milestone was the advent of the official "Roast." While they had the concept in place for decades, it wasn't until they woke up from their slumber of slumps that the Roast really took hold. They realized that their lavish, sophisticated dinners had begun to resemble a cross between a Soupy Sales *Stop Me if You've Heard It* show and a *Playboy After Dark* segment. So around the halfway mark in the century they decided that along with their new digs, new members, and a new beginning, they would start a new format, and so the Roast was born.

According to Buddy Arnold, who produced many dinners and Roasts, "The Friars Club did not originate Roasts. Saints and Sinners originated Roasts in the late 1800s, but their Roasts were not dirty Roasts. Those Roasts were open to men and women, saints and sinners. The Friars Roast was started by Milton in the '50s and was made a little different in that it was only stag. Being only stag, it took on a different connotation and flavor in the type of thing it became: dirty language. Dirt, clever dirt, will get you a bigger laugh."

Harry Delf, working in tandem with Berle to foster the Friars' new unique event, certainly saw it as a labor of love in spite of the fact that his personality was directly opposite the format. As Harry Delf, Jr. relates, it was the lean times that forced the Friars to search for new and innovative ways to survive. "My father got the money by coming up with the idea of reinstituting these dinners as

Roasts," he says. "He was on the dais on every one of them. He wasn't on the dais in the sense that he made a presentation, but he always was the person who introduced and started these Roasts. He was the first speaker and they used to kid him because he was always boring. He didn't come up with anything crazy. A dirty word out of my father's mouth was impossible, so they always used to tease him. But he always played a back seat because he felt that he wasn't well known enough to get the attraction necessary to get the club going."

In spite of Delf's reserved manner, he did agree to an official Roast himself. "I remember the one they had for my father, when Jack E. Leonard did such a number on him I got up and left," recalls Harry Delf, Jr. "I was standing in the back and Jack E. Leonard was vicious beyond belief. He always was that way, but he was hitting my father on every single button you can imagine, so I just got up and left. I didn't go to most of them because my father didn't want his son hearing all that. It sounds funny now, but he was that kind of a guy. He was on the prudish side."

Richard Lewis supports the Roast form of flattery that is so unique to this institution. "They're indigenous to the Friars Club," he explains. "Look, sometimes they get insanely hilarious, sometimes they get insanely nasty, but you know what? The bottom line, when you blend them all together, it's a big part of comedy history."

Comedy sage Red Buttons agrees. "All this stuff was done so many years ago," he says. "All these dinners and all these Roasts—of course they're planned. They're not rehearsed, but they're planned. People talk to one another and put things together."

Judy Gold concurs, having performed at the Rob Reiner and Smothers Brothers Roasts.

Milton Berle, Chico Marx, Pat O'Brien, and Ted Lewis at the Friars Club Roast of Phil Silvers — 1951

"Preparing for the Roast, it is so much work. It's really a collaborative thing," she says. "You realize that other comics in the Friars Club, especially when you're doing a Roast, they're so giving. I felt like that when I was preparing for the Roast, that I could really call these guys and say, 'Help me—what do you think of this?'"

Buttons says, "From the performer's standpoint, it's preparation that's the romance of this thing. Sitting down and blocking it out and knowing who they're talking about and doing a background on the 'victims,' if they're being roasted. But people do this in our business. I mean, actors do it when they go in to do a role if they're playing somebody else, especially a person who had been alive on this mortal coil. They'll get into the

specifics; they'll get all the information they possibly can. Well, the same thing with us, even though it's not in the acting genre. The more information you have, the more you have to cull from.

"You have to do fresh material. That's the one thing I did right through my whole career of doing all that stuff for the New York Friars. It was fresh as a daisy every time I came up. Every time I took a shot out of the box on the dais I came in fresh." Buttons is proof that fresh *and* funny rule at the Friars!

Norm Crosby, a Roast pro, acknowledges that there is more to this format than meets the eye: "You're not going to do your act, because it's a totally different environment. It's learning a little bit about the guest of honor. You can take the oldest joke in the world, but if it fits that person, it works. And you can be risqué, you can be dirty, but it just has to belong. It has to fit. And that's the secret. If you sit down and figure out four, five minutes that belong to that guy, belong to that afternoon, to that crowd."

But then again, there's Henny Youngman, who even Crosby cuts some slack in the Roast preparation game: "Henny would get up, an hour. 'I was walking down the street the other day, and my wife said....' He would have nothing to do with the guy! He's standing right next to him, and the man would not even look at him. And everyone would laugh because Henny could get away with it. But if you do a Roast and you're supposed to roast

somebody, you don't just get up and do five minutes of your act!" Unless of course, you're Henny.

Jan Murray also knows how to circumnavigate the treacherous Roast waters. "I always had a theme, and if the theme plays, then it's great," he says. "It's hysterical. If the theme dies, I die. You have to understand, you have no place to break these things in. You write them and you go on. You've got material, you don't know if it's funny. You're alone in a room. You need an audience to know if they're going to laugh or not. So, if I have a whole chunk, a whole routine—I'm not talking about one-line jokes now, one-line jokes are recognizable to me right away and to any comedian— I'm talking about themed things. If they don't buy

Martha Raye at her Roast before the barbs flew—1954

the theme, I don't care how funny you are, you're not going to get any laughs."

LeRoy Neiman is often on the receiving end of Friars jokes at their Roasts, thanks to his artistry as well as his trademark bushy mustache. "I take it as a terrific compliment," he says. "I take it like when you finally qualified to be called a 'bum' by Toots Shor you were in. An insult from a highly personal viewpoint of your shortcomings and cleverly put, whatever it is, it's a compliment coming from the right person. Nobody else would do that."

THE EVOLUTION OF THE DAIS

These Roasts and testimonial dinners do not just suddenly appear. As Jean-Pierre Trebot explains, "I don't think people realize the time and energy that is expended to put these events together." The audience comes to these fancy affairs, they enjoy cocktails and are privy to the crème

Sammy Davis, Jr. is brought to tears at his Friars Club Roast. It wouldn't be the last time that would happen to a guest of honor. Harry Delf and Red Buttons are witnesses — 1956

de la crème of show biz, but it doesn't happen overnight. Celebrities are wooed, coddled, and cajoled. You think superstars are sitting at home just waiting to be called and asked if the Friars can eviscerate their egos for a "fun" event?

As Trebot notes, "There have been some very valuable Friars who have taken great pains to present to the members—and the world at large—brilliant productions. And these events are as complicated as any Hollywood showcase. Friars like Buddy Arnold, David Tebet, Robert Saks, Ken Greengrass, John Schreiber, and Mark Krantz have put us on the map with their shows. They are to be commended for their loyalty and dedication to the club in putting together quality events."

After more than fifty years of the official Roast

creation, some comics still won't go near it, although some, like Richard Lewis, have very valid reasons. "The one type of event which is most famous for the Friars, which are the Roasts, is the event that I purposefully have a problem doing," Lewis says. "There's a real reason for it—my whole thing as a standup comedian is talking about me. I didn't develop a hook like Red Buttons, which is brilliant and genius—'never had a dinner.' I just never developed that hook to be able to be comfortable enough to get out of my own skin.

"I'm the same person on stage as I am off, and I just never figured out a way to affectionately berate anyone else but me. Don Rickles and Belzer and Gilbert Gottfried, those kinds of guys can do this in their sleep, and I'm leaving out many, obvi-

YOUNG AT HEART

For George Jessel's birthday dinner party held at the 56th Street clubhouse, sung by Frank Sinatra, written by Milton Berle and Buddy Arnold.

Fairy tales all came true
For this jolly green Jew
Who is young at heart!
On the day of his bris
Georgie planted a kiss
On his nurse's heart!
And at five, unafraid
He molested his maid
And at nine, where he stayed
He got caught in a raid!
In school, he taught his teacher
All the facts of life
In "shul" they caught him "clyding"
With the Rabbi's wife!

That was back in the past
But the track is still fast
He's over sixty-five!
And he's still full of fight
Drinking Pepsi all night
Just to come alive!
Life's a drag when he's stag
Sex to him is no gag
Though I don't like to brag
Next to him I'm a fag!

Georgie, long may you swing
You're the ring-a-ding king
Of romantic art
From the chicks you now date
Back to Catherine the great
You have done your part

So we hope you survive
To a hundred-and-five
'Cause there's no one alive
With your strength and your drive

You fabulous Friar
When you retire
Your picture will be hung
Among the young at heart!

ously. But these are the guys who are brilliant at it. I am far better at putting myself down. One of the reasons I went on stage is because I felt I was being put down, so the last thing I like to do is get up on stage and destroy somebody."

Rickles humbly concurs: "I think when I'm on the dais for roasting, I usually come off very well. I can't say I'm the greatest one of all, no. But I think I suit Roasts. I fit like a glove when it comes to comedy Roasts."

While Lewis has his reasons for not being a roaster, he could handle being on the receiving end. "One day I hope I get the honor to be roasted—'take my *life*, please!'" he says. "That would be a pleasure, and hopefully one day it will happen. They'll have a field day because I'm a basket case and they all know it."

Not everyone agrees, however, so don't ask John Travolta to be subjected to a Roast. "If you look at Hope, Carson, Shecky Greene, the '50s and early '60s roasting, it had a spirit of play and they had a lot of fun. Even an early Don Rickles," Travolta says. "But what happens is that out of moves of desperateness, over the years, to get funnier and funnier, it got lower and deeper and much more stinging and much less fun. So, you want to avoid them.

"They get so personal. It's not, 'Gee, you have a big nose and isn't this fun.' Now it goes right to the quick and you go, 'Oh, God, why did they go there?' It's like that one friend that everyone might have growing up that just has to tell you the truth and they tell you the truth that is really rough on you. But you kind of go, 'Okay, that's their nature.' It's only one in the group and they only do it on occasion. Here, it's like in front of millions."

Jack L. Green, the dean emeritus of the Friars, describes those early events as he talks about his

Jack Benny and Ed McMahon trying to see eye to eye—1950s

first Roast. "Joe E. Lewis at the Hotel Astor, that's where they used to run the events," Green remembers. "It was very different. There were no women at all at the event. It was purely men. The dais, unlike the daises today, only had eight people on it. But each one had a microphone in front of him and there was nothing prepared, and they would just throw barbs at each other. Somebody would say something and they'd get up or Groucho Marx would get up and say something and then they would really roast each other. And it was fun; it was off the top of their heads. It was non-rehearsed and it was just instantaneous laughs."

But things have changed since those simple times, as Green says: "Today the dais is not made up of only comedians anymore. There are celebrities of all types. They don't have that same way of delivering lines or the same rapport with the guest of honor

that the fellow comics had. As if you would have a dancer being honored and all the other dancers would have something in common, so it works differently. Plus the fact that the more people on the dais, the longer the dais, and the longer the dais, the more front-row tables you sell. So it's a question of economics as well."

For first-time Friars, experiencing the Roast from the audience's viewpoint is quite an experience. "I was sitting in the audience and we had, to my taste, a very sumptuous lunch, and then they passed out cigars," says Norm Crosby. "I didn't even smoke—I was sick as a dog. I was puffing on the cigar, getting dizzy. I think it was Nat King Cole's Roast and Jessel was on the dais and Henny Youngman—people who I had never dreamt I would see in person. Johnny Carson, God! These were legends—and, of course, Milton. Somebody said something, I think Jessel was speaking, and then Youngman interrupted him and said something and Jessel turned around and said, 'Shut the fuck up!' And I went right off my chair. Right on the floor! I said, 'Did you hear what he said?' And everyone at the table said, 'That's nothing. This is a Friars Roast—wait 'til you hear what they say.' I was in total shock. I couldn't believe it. And then of course I became a roaster. I became a member of the family."

Ed McMahon also got an earful at his first Roast. "I went into a luncheon—it was for Georgie Jessel, so that goes way back—that's an early one of the Roasts," McMahon says. "It was a closed luncheon, males only in those days. The biggest shock of my life was to hear Jack Benny, who was on the microphone, telling a story about George Jessel, and he used very, very salty language. For me, Jack Benny was my idol, as well as Johnny's idol. The fact that here was my idol, on a microphone, saying words that you heard in a locker room or on a football field, it just blew me away. It was so mind-boggling."

Jerry Stiller admits that, for this reason, he didn't attend many Roasts. "Alan King said when they made me the roastee, that you can't say fuck in front of Jerry Stiller, there'd be a meltdown," he says. "I had a big problem with listening to the words. I said, 'Why do they have to talk like that?' I made these comics like my grandfathers; I revered them. Yet at these Roasts, when they said things like that, it really affected me in such a way that I said I can't go there because I would blush. I'd turn red. I'm really a prude. I don't use four-letter words on stage, but in real life I do. I also play characters who are off the wall. That goes deep. At the same time I still wanted to be one of the boys. So you can't go around saying, 'I'm gonna reform the Friars.'

"I went to a Roast, I was sitting with Howard Cosell, and they were honoring Tommy LaSorda. I had a great time listening to Howard talk, and I said to him at one point, 'Howard, how can you be so outspoken?' And he said, 'Because I know I'm right!' I guess I missed a lot in my life."

For LeRoy Neiman even Roasts can be classy affairs. "I was at some pretty rough Roasts when Henny and those guys were around," Neiman says. "The jokes were more classic, you might say. When I came, there was still the feeling of Jolson and all those kinds of people. In my work, I've had to make

adjustments to subject matter and different things. In football I go back practically to the leather helmet—I go back to the baseball shoes and all that kind of stuff. But you can never omit what's happening; you have to absorb it. You can't say, 'Well I don't like that—it's not what it should be,' because that's the way it is. If you're creating something that is expressing yourself, you've got to realize that people living today are gonna look at it."

Pat Cooper was nonplussed by this new Roast experience. "The language never threw me because I was always such a filthy mouth anyway," he explains. "I heard words that weren't invented yet in those days, but that didn't bother me. It was just sitting there with a nice suit and everything— it was like going into the ocean with a tuxedo on." He also says there is an art to closing a Roast—an art that Cooper mastered, becoming a staple at the Roasts as the comic who went on last.

"This didn't happen right away," he says. "How did they know if I could handle it? I did Rich Little's Roast and whatever I said must have been funny. Then the next year, I think it was Jerry Lewis, they turned around and they said, 'Pat, you're gonna go on last.' I said, 'What, go on last? What are you people, nuts?' But I wouldn't give in to say I can't do it. First I thought they were trying to torture me. I think they were out to get me, but I survived and I was very fortunate. I said, 'Boy, I got through that one.'

"Then also the next year I got to go again, and I go, 'God Almighty, it's really a pressure cooker.' Because you're with people paying top dollar, you're with great entertainers on that dais, and they're all gonna say 99 percent of what you were ready to say—and you're last. So I learned what you could not say. I listened to what everybody said, and I said, 'Well, now I can't say that.' So

Milton Berle's bachelor dinner at the Waldorf Astoria Hotel — 1953

what I did was I always had a backup: In case I couldn't say enough about the guy being roasted, I went after somebody else. And I said to myself, 'That's got to be the ticket.' I try to tell some of these younger kids to do that, and they go, 'Why would you do that?' and I go, 'You're missing the point, that's what makes you funny.' I said, 'If you're doing Richard Pryor, and you got nothing to say about him, you say, 'You know something, Richie, you aggravate me. I'm gonna go after so and so,' and that's what closing is all about."

FROM BERLE TO BOGIE

In 1953 the Friars held a stag dinner for Milton Berle. Actually, the Friars probably held about ten thousand dinners and Roasts for Berle during his long tenure. Jan Murray recalls: "Well, I did fifty for Milton. If you give him a plaque, he comes to your house and does twenty minutes. Every Thursday we were roasting him and honoring him." This partic-

ular honor was held as his bachelor party, weeks before his wedding to Ruth.

"I was there," says Buddy Arnold. "This was one of the funniest affairs I've ever been to in my life. I was hoarse from laughing. I wrote a lot of stuff for that. It was a stag Roast. Everything filthy, but real funny filth. It wasn't just for the stage. These guys don't need shock value out of filth.

"Everybody that was big in New York at the time was there, and Milton's future father-in-law, Ruth's father, laughed the hardest of all. When it was all over several of us went over to Lindy's to meet Ruth and her mother, who were waiting for her father. Milton and myself and Goodman Ace, who was one of the greatest comedy writers of all time, walked into Lindy's. We saw Ruth and her mother sitting there, and Goody Ace called across to the table, 'Hi, Ruth. We were just talking about you.'

"Also, Jesse Block was in the house. A great story he told about a trip with George Burns and

Phil Silvers, Joe E. Lewis, Lauren Bacall, and Humphrey Bogart at the Friars Roast of Humphrey Bogart — 1955

Jack Benny. They got in the car on the West Coast to drive to the East Coast. The three of them were going to go cross-country in the car. George Burns was driving. So, Burns picks up Jesse Block, and then he goes to get Jack Benny, and then they were going to go from there. They park to pick up Benny, and Benny says to Jesse, 'You don't mind if I sit on the outside? I have to get out first at the Essex House.'"

Little did the Friars know that in 1955 when they roasted Humphrey Bogart, the tape from this event would be copied and bootlegged more than a Paris Hilton video. Red Buttons speaks of being the evening's roastmaster: "My opening salvo was something that really established me in the stag Roast field as one of the luminaries. When I sucked them in, telling him what a fan I was, and how I've seen all his pictures and how thrilled I am to be the master of ceremonies today. That I've seen your movies five and six times apiece, but my favorite was the one in the South Pacific, where

you landed on this island and you jumped off the barge with guns blazing. The bodies were piled up, and when you ran out of bullets you pulled out a knife, you slashed flesh, you shimmied up a tree, you threw down snipers, you jumped on a tank, you opened the turret, you threw in a hand grenade, you exploded the tank. I said, 'Mr. Bogart, do you remember doing that?' And he looked up at me, he was just watching me right through the whole thing, and he just looked up at me, and he said, 'Yes, I do.' I said, 'You're full of shit. That was John Wayne.' Well, that was one of the most explosive laughs I have ever heard."

The Bogart Roast was memorable for Jan Murray, as well. "The first one I did was the one with Humphrey Bogart," he recalls. "I had never done a Friars Roast before. "When I got up, I said, 'I don't know why I'm here. I don't remember you from the mountains. Did you ever work at Kutsher's Country Club?' I was doing odd things from the Catskills mountains for him. I mean, he's Humphrey Bogart! The audience screamed. They loved that. I said, 'Why would I know you? Did you work at Brown's Hotel?' He was like the top star in the world, and I'm asking him about the mountains, if we ever worked the Catskills together."

Lauren Bacall made Friars history by roasting her husband via a tape recording. She called the Friars "rat bastards" for not letting her roast along with the guys, telling the crowd what she said to Bogey when he told her she wasn't allowed to go: "What the hell can the Friars say that you haven't called me?" They did, however, let her come out after the arrows had been slung, and hopefully stung, to be there when Bogart accepted his Friars cufflinks from Buttons and Abbot Joe E. Lewis.

Gene Baylos took a page out of Henny Youngman's tips on roasting: "I'll tell you the truth:

I don't know Humphrey Bogart, so fuck him. I didn't come here to make with the jokes. The real truth is, the car's going to Jersey, and the game starts in the afternoon. I just played a hotel in Miami Beach, the Fontainebleau, fabulous hotel. It's a little overdone. They have an eight-piece band playing in the men's room. I think all they need is a piano and a violin—that's enough. There's no room to dance." Gene ended with, "Do you ever get the feeling you're in the wrong business?" In spite of his ignoring the guest of honor, Gene was one of

a kind and definitely in the right business.

MARILYN AND LIZ

Jerry Lewis and Dean Martin were honored with a dinner in 1955. This star-studded dais had one standout star—the only woman on the dais. Now, admittedly, even Ruth Buzzi would stand out in those odds, but this particular woman had the men saying, "To hell with Jerry and Dino." Milton Berle remembered: "If you could picture everybody in dinner jackets, including myself, and one woman in the

Clockwise from above: Program from the Dean Martin and Jerry Lewis Friars Club dinner in 1955.

Martin, Milton Berle, and Lewis share the stage at the dinner.

The trio clowns with Marilyn Monroe at the dinner.

middle: Marilyn Monroe. We didn't do anything rough on her or anything. We weren't that dirty or saying four-letter words or anything like that."

Henny Youngman kept the Marilyn theme up when he did his turn at the dais. Knowing full well he wouldn't be saying much about the guests of honor, he said: "A movie fan in the Bronx always faints when he sees a Marilyn Monroe picture, and keeps hollering, 'Seltzer! Seltzer!' Ushers could

understand the fainting, but why holler 'seltzer'? 'I get thirsty also when I faint,' he explained."

Ed Sullivan was a very brave man. He chose to dedicate one of his television shows to a Friars Roast in his honor. In 1958 when America tuned in to his popular variety show on CBS, they were treated to real Friars making real Roast jokes—only these were clean. Joe E. Lewis, Walter Cronkite, Jack Carter, Jack E. Leonard, Joey Bishop, Morey Amsterdam, and Phil Silvers were on the dais, throwing out comments left and right. Poor Ed didn't know what hit him. Neither did the viewing audience.

"It was very good and very sharp," says Buddy Arnold, "and show business people knew what it meant—that you were insulting someone with love. The public wasn't aware of it in those days. They took it on the nose. Everything that was said, they didn't see the humor in it. So consequently, the next day in the paper there were all kinds of letters: 'How could you do a thing to such a man?' They were not inculcated to the beauty and the love that went into these things. It took a long time for the public to realize that this was dedicated to an individual through respect, mostly respect. In fact, Don Rickles wasn't understood right away when he went into show business. Don would insult people from the floor. That's a form of Roast. But when Don would insult people like Frank Sinatra, the public would see Sinatra laughing at insults thrown at

Eddie Fisher, Eva Sully, and Elizabeth Taylor at a Friars Club testimonial dinner — 1960s

himself. They started to come around and understand a little bit about what a Roast was."

March 23, 1958, was supposed to be an exciting day for the Friars, Mike Todd, and his wife, Elizabeth Taylor. That was the day they would have honored the show business mogul and producer of the hit film *Around the World in Eighty Days.* Todd's plane crashed on his way from California to New York to attend the dinner (Elizabeth Taylor stayed home sick with a bad cold).

Buddy Arnold was a producer of that event: "Our committee met. We said, 'What are we going to do? We've got all these tickets sold.' The Friars Club depends on this money. This was our big annual affair that year. I said, 'Assuming she'll do it, why don't we ask Elizabeth if a month or two from now, whenever she feels comfortable, we roast him posthumously. But she's his representative; she'll sit at the table for him.' They thought it was a bad idea, very poor taste.

"We never asked her. We did a Frolics instead. I found out subsequently that she would have been extremely happy to have done it, because she felt that it might have been a big honor for him. He always boasted to her about the Friars and what it meant to him. She said, 'I would have done it dedicated to his memory.'"

WHAT KIND OF FOOL AM I?

From the Friars Club "Beat the Press" dinner, sung by Sammy Davis, Jr., written by Milton Berle and Buddy Arnold.

What kind of fool am I?
To waste my time at stags
When I could be with Pat and Dick
Instead of with these four fags!

What can they do for us?
These aging schmucks
We should have Rona Barrett here
At least she sucks!

What kind of fool am I?
To honor these four shits?
Each time they mention blacks
These friggin' hacks
Play favorites

They quote Flip Wilson's bits
And Belafonte's hits
But not one line about
The tits of Eartha Kitt's

I speak for ev'ry Friar
You assholes should retire
Give up your phony tricks
And all those slick reporting schticks

You should be in *Deep Throat*
Because you're four big pricks!

CHAPTER FOUR

THOSE LOVABLE, LAUGHABLE, LEWDABLE FRIARS

Events in the '60s and '70s

Opposite page: The best pie-throwers since Soupy Sales—the Friars—pelt the picture of Don Rickles at his testimonial dinner—1974

A legend both inside and outside of the Friars Club, George Burns lasted a hundred years—which gave the Friars plenty of time to honor him. In 1960 his cronies got together and threw him a stag Roast. It was held at the Astor Hotel and George Jessel helmed the proceedings. "There was a great dinner given here last night, and deservedly so, in honor of Jack Benny," Jessel began. "The March of Dimes humanitarian award was given to him. And I still have some stuff left over from last night—and the lunch that you had was also left over from last night. Last night, the great artist Danny Kaye made a speech that, had you come in in the middle of it, you would have thought it was the circumcision of Queen Elizabeth's new baby."

Dave Barry also delivered comments about Burns. "The

first time I met George was at a synagogue in Beverly Hills," Barry said. "I figured if I could eavesdrop on his prayers, maybe he would ad-lib and I could pick up a one-liner. But I couldn't hear a thing, because frankly one member was in the back row singing so loudly that finally I had to turn around and say, 'Sammy!'"

Harry Herschfield had been a staple at Friars events since the 48th Street monastery. Here's a Herschfield joke from the Burns Roast: "I went to dinner with a guy one night, and he took me to some place, and the food was the worst. I never ate such lousy meat in my life. I couldn't eat it, so he said, 'Send it back.' I said, 'No, I'll cut it up a little bit and give it to my dog tonight.' So I took it home, gave it to my dog. The next day he said, 'How'd the dog like the meat?' I said, 'He ate every bit of it. When he finished, he started licking his ass to take the taste out of his mouth.'"

Al Bernie also spoke at the Roast and gave the guest of honor this advice: "If we look at the history of George Burns, it is the history of show business. He was in vaudeville before it died. He was in radio before it died. He was in television— George, there are only a couple of nightclubs left in the country. Stay out!"

Jack Benny took the dais late in the evening. "After listening to all of these alleged comedians,"

he said, "I have come to one decision: I am not going to change my delivery. As a rule at these stag dinners, they always pay me this sort of left-handed compliment by putting me on very late. This can either be a compliment or an insult. Of course, the compliment being that if they put me on very early, nobody will be able to follow me. And the insult being that we better get the show rolling before Benny gets on, and so far this afternoon's been rolling in shit."

Norm Crosby heard about this gem from Benny: "You know, Jack said at the George Burns Roast, 'I've never heard George use profanity. Well, except one time he was playing bridge and he called his partner a fucking imbecile. Now, how anyone in the world would call Irene Dunn a fucking imbecile'— and then he took a pause and he said, 'Well, maybe she is.' From Jack Benny! It was brilliant."

While Don Rickles was in attendance at this Roast, he didn't perform. His time in the roaster chair had not yet come. He was up-and-coming at this time, but already his reputation had preceded him, and he was told by Jessel to just sit there and keep his mouth shut. "I was the new kid on the block," Rickles explains. "Being different, making fun of everybody was received just beautifully. They really gave me a reputation. Every time I got up on the Roasts it was important, because I was someone who was different. And the people of the Friars Club were great to me."

Nothing gave George Burns more pleasure than a Jack Benny story, so during his speech he had this to share: "Last night I spoke at the Jack Benny dinner. That was quite an affair. Mrs.

Harry Herschfield, George Burns, Jack Benny, and Phil Silvers laugh it up at the Friars Club's George Burns Roast—1960

Steve Allen, Joe E. Lewis, and Jayne Meadows having a few laughs at a Friars event—1960s

Roosevelt, Helen Hayes, Senator Javits, a dais full of celebrities, and Jack got nervous. He whispered to me, 'George, this is a high-class affair, nothing risqué.' I said, 'Should I tell the story about Sid Gary's ass?' He said, 'I wouldn't if I was you, because Javits is on ahead of you, and he's telling it.'"

ONE OF THEIR OWN

If George M. Cohan was the rock the early Friars held firmly onto, Joe E. Lewis was the glue that held the Friars together in the middle of the century. "The greatest was Joe E. Lewis," Alan King fondly recalls. "He's the one who is least remem-

Harry Delf presents Joe E. Lewis with his gift for being roasted — 1962

bered. He was abbot for a very long time. He never had a movie career, never had a television career. He was the last of the great nightclub comedians. When he got sick and Frank Sinatra and the whole gang rushed him to the hospital, everybody was very concerned. He lived a long time after that, but at that time, we didn't know. He said to Sinatra on the way to surgery, 'What's the prognosis? Don't bullshit me.' Frank said, 'Well, you've got about a fifty-fifty chance.' He said, 'Get me out of here. I want better odds.' And everybody laughed."

LeRoy Neiman used to hang out with Joe E. either at the monastery or at Toots Shor's. "After the fights usually we'd go late to Toots, and Toots would drink his fifth of brandy, and everybody would drink, and sometimes the fighters would come briefly," Neiman says. "As the morning wound down, three o'clock, Joe E. Lewis was still

holding court at the table—they had a round table there. Joe E. would talk about this guy, about that guy, so he had something for everybody at the table—and he worked the whole table. Then he'd just pass out, and one night I had the honor of taking him home in a cab from Toots and handing him to the doorman. I got the honor. I was highly complimented, with this guy that was laid out next to me in the back seat. But that kind of stuff, that's only the Friars."

Freddie Roman tells of spending one very special evening with Joe E.: "I met him one night in my life. I was new at the club and just starting to make a little bit of noise, and I get a booking at an old nightclub in New York called The Living Room. I was the headliner, and on the second show on Wednesday night—I'll never forget it—my friend John Delustro was friendly with Joe E. Lewis, and he brought him to my second show. After the show was over I went to his table, we sat there 'til three in the morning. He was telling me how wonderful I did but maybe that joke you did at the beginning should go later on, and he was trying to be most helpful. It was a wonderful, wonderful evening. My God, an idol—and the abbot of the club! He said, 'You gotta join the Friars.' I said, 'I did, six months ago.' He said, 'Good, we'll have a drink at the bar.' And I never saw him again. But he was most helpful."

Alan King says of Joe E.: "He was the kindest man, and he'd stand right at the corner of the bar, and everybody would sit around, and he could tell stories. The first time I met Joe E., at the Friars, I was just a kid and I'm working a bust-out joint in Atlantic City, a long time ago. I did the worst first show. It was a wise-guy joint. I didn't even wait. I just put my coat on. I left. I didn't want to go back, because I just knew I was going to get thrown out. Joe E. was working the 500 Club, and he had on his tuxedo between shows. I see him and he says, 'Hey, kid! So, what happened?' I tell him I'm afraid to go back. He went to a pay phone and he called my club. He called the boss—Three Fingers, whatever they called him. He said, 'I hear you got my kid Alan King working for you. Listen, hold the second show. I'm coming over.' He brought about fifteen people. So, with Joe E. Lewis coming to see me, I wasn't going to get fired when I got back. Then I got lucky—I got funny. So I stayed in the joint for about four weeks, but I always remember Joe E. He was a very kind man.

"I once saw him give a bust-out guy a hundred dollars. I said, 'Joe E., what the hell is the matter with you?' He says, 'For a hundred dollars, do you want to destroy a legend?' He didn't give a shit. When he got sick, he lived at the Warwick Hotel at the end of his life, and he used to take that long walk here to the club. We were in this building already. He'd sit and play gin, and we'd walk him back. He was a great fellow. Absolutely great fellow."

If this man didn't deserve a Friars honor then nobody did. In 1962 they held a testimonial dinner in Joe E.'s honor, with Milton Berle as the master of ceremonies. In spite of their having already made the distinction between Roasts and dinners, they seemed to have harkened back to their old ways—roasting in tuxedos.

Among Jack Carter's comments that night were: "Joe E. was with me last year on this very night, when I got married. I'm married just a year ago tonight, so it's kind of an anniversary, and my little bride is here. Will you take a little bow, so they know I'm still with you? Joe E. came to the wedding in Miami. He took time off from his drunk and track duty. It was a lovely affair—and they nearly threw him out. He was stone drunk, and when he hit the door two cops said to him, 'What side are you on, the bride or the groom?' And he said 'You schmuck, I'm with the caterer.' And now he's sitting on the aisle with my mother and father and as I said to the rabbi, 'I do,' he says, 'Ah, I blew another bet.' Then he threw losing tickets at us."

Berle's comment to Carter was, "Jack, you said some of the funniest things that I'll ever use."

Myron Cohen said, "I worship the very ground this man walks on. If Miriam would divorce me, and I was a girl, and Joe would have me, my name would be Mrs. Joe E. Lewis."

Steve Lawrence, Jean Carroll, and Georgie Price sang a parody of "There's No Business like Show Business":

There's no business like Joe's business
We all start with a joke
We're the ones that Joe E. always pays off
And he's never used an I.O.U.
Maybe never had too many days off
'Cause when he lays off
We lay off too

There's no bankroll like Joe's bankroll
He's so free with his dough
At the mutual window he supports the track
If he stops drinking, I'll get the sack
When he reaches eighty I'll be flat on my back
There's no sucker like Joe

Jack E. Leonard threw out a few one-liners: "Chubby Checker is here. Up 'til tonight I though Chubby Checker was a cab. . . . Phil Silvers and I ought to put our heads together—we'll look like Jane Mansfield."

If you thought that no way would Liberace ever be at a Friars Club event, guess again. Before he

Friars Club dinner in honor of Dinah Shore, with George Montgomery and Red Buttons — 1960

played "Piano Blues," he noted, "Glad you noticed the outfit. I only wore it once before, at the Royal command performance, in London, for Queen Elizabeth. And I thought I'd wear it again tonight, for a command performance for the king of all nightclub comics, Joe E. Lewis. The only difference between my clothes and Joe E. Lewis's is mine are deductible from my income tax." When he exited Joe E. shouted out, "And you thought I was drunk!"

If you ever wondered if the lovable but narcissistic television character Sgt. Bilko was an exact replica of Phil Silvers, the man who made him famous, just take a look at his comments: "Everybody, of course, loves Joe E., and that leaves so little to say except to be redundant. That he loves me more than anybody in the room is just a tribute to my own personal charm. It is a happy

paradox that a man whose career has been built on booze, broads, and gambling is, in essence and in honesty, the most decent man I have ever known in show business."

It seemed fitting to close Joe E.'s dinner with the man who started the memories flowing. Alan King closed the show that night in 1962 with: "Every joke I ever thought of, every joke I ever wished I'd thought of, has already been said. Being raised in an Orthodox home, I realized that my father and my rabbi were liars. Because here was a man who defied Moses and became a success, and I said, 'That's good enough for me.' I worship this man. I sat at his feet. I thought, if I could ever learn to be what Joe E. Lewis is—in fact, when I'm through with this speech, I want to accept the award, 'cause I've sat as long as he has and I haven't had as much fun. He's beautiful. I'm very happy to be here."

THE RAT PACK

The Nat King Cole Roast that Norm Crosby attended in 1964 was a rare treat, owing to the fact that singers were usually spared from these bawdy events. Crooners, for the most part, were relegated to the more honorable testimonial dinners, so Cole was a brave soul for agreeing to it. But according to the *Friars Fables*, a club newsletter that was published during times when *The Epistle* was not, "Cole took a fair share of four letters in what was probably one of the more gentle ribfests in recent years. It was a session with its quota of questionable words, but somehow the barbs were without rancor."

George Jessel, as roastmaster, started off by sharing the singer's beginnings, telling tales of his early days as a choirboy on the East side back when he was known as Nathan Cohen. Jessel then stated that he had to fly out immediately afterward for a dinner in California that evening and would speak at a birth the following morning. "The same speech will be given in all three places," he joked.

Nipsey Russell described Cole as the man who brought jazz up the river from New Orleans. "He couldn't get on a bus," Russell joked.

When Johnny Carson took the podium, he was kind to Cole but described the made-in-Israel watch that Jessel had given him: "It is now ten minutes before two. In another hour it will be ten minutes to one."

The Friars gave Nat a set of golf clubs that included a gold putter with the Friars insignia and a set of gold tees. Don't tell the current roastees, though, since they now just get a statue that is more like a little Friar doorstop.

Sammy Davis, Jr. was brave enough to agree to

Al Kelly contemplating some liquid assistance to get through his Friars Club Roast — 1966

Jan Murray and Abbe Lane at Joey Bishop's testimonial dinner — 1964

a dinner in 1966. Then again, when you're a member of the Rat Pack, why not accept the honor since it's a given that somebody is going to have your back? The problem with this event was that there weren't any fellow Rat Packers around to do that. Granted, it was a testimonial, but you would think these honorees would have learned by then that with the Friars there really wasn't that much of a difference between the tone at their Roasts and at their other signature events.

"Sammy Davis," said Steve Lawrence, "lived one of the great love stories of history. He saw what he wanted and he went after it. And Sammy, I hope you and Frank Sinatra will be very happy together." Lawrence also commented on the recent cancella-

tions of their TV shows: "Now that you're Jewish, remember our age-old prayer: 'Let our people go.' Well, our prayer has been answered. CBS let me go—and NBC has let you go."

New York City Mayor John Lindsay presented Sammy with a proclamation on behalf of the city, quipping: "You represent the most compact minority group in town."

A couple of the dais members were not spared, as evidenced when Toastmaster Johnny Carson said to one of them, "Senator Javits is evidently interested in President Johnson's job. He was seen at the synagogue Friday night wearing a ten-gallon yarmulke." Robert Kennedy was also in attendance to support Sammy, but being a good friend

Eydie Gorme, Diahann Carroll, Sidney Poitier, and Buddy Howe at the Friars Club dinner in honor of Sammy Davis, Jr. — 1966

meant nothing to Jackie Vernon, who turned to the senator and said, "Senator, you're not supposed to doze off, you know." But Kennedy laughed so he must have been sleeping with one eye open.

Sammy was humbled by all the accolades and, as one reporter wrote, "Sammy Davis explained his incessant drive, his way of life, his sacrifices, and his philosophy last night. 'I am trying to get even,' the idolized Sammy set forth. Then he elaborated that he was constantly trying to get even for the debt he owed others for making his magnificent world of stardom and friendship possible." Okay, so maybe he didn't need his back covered after all.

ROASTING RICKLES

Jack E. Leonard was roastmaster when that new kid on the block, Don Rickles, was roasted in 1968. "I don't mind the guy stealing my act," said Leonard at that event, "but he stole my hair, too!"

Apparently the years helped Rickles to think back fondly on that Roast, and he says, "Jack E. Leonard was a great star and a great friend. And he insisted I was doing him, which wasn't the case, but who's going to argue? Jackie's now in a

Senators Jacob Javits and Robert Kennedy most likely are not discussing politics at the Friars Club dinner in honor of Sammy Davis, Jr. — 1966

Don Rickles enjoys a few laughs at his expense from Jack E. Leonard at the Friars Roast of Don Rickles — 1968

better world, and I'm not going to pick on him. All I can say it was great fun, and Jackie was a top guy in what he did."

The Rickles Roast was the first one during which Norm Crosby performed as a roaster. "I remember that Jack E. Leonard was the emcee and he totally intimidated me. He was so powerful," Crosby says. "He turned to Ed Sullivan and said, 'Was the ground cold when you got up this morning?' For no reason! He just said it to him. And Sullivan stood up—and nobody ever heard Sullivan say bad words. Sullivan, no matter who was being roasted, would always say, 'It's good to be here. Sylvia sends her love. Good luck to you,' and he'd sit down. No matter who it was. And he stood up and said, 'Fuck you,' and the crowd went nuts."

Crosby's first time as a member on the Friars' firing squad of wits almost never happened. "One of the roasters said something and started to get mixed up and goofed. Jackie said, 'You've been talking to Norm Crosby,' and everybody laughed," Crosby recalls. "Well, because he said my name, he told me afterwards, for some reason he thought that I'd been on, and so he went down the whole list of people and skipped me. When he was winding up, he said, 'And now, Buddy Howe will present the Friars statue.' And somebody said to him, 'You didn't introduce Norm Crosby!' It was a terrible spot because it was over! I said, 'If this is a test!' and I went up and I said, 'Thanks, Jack. It's

such a thrill to be ignored by you.' Whatever I said, they laughed. I did five minutes, and it was wonderful, and then I sat down. But I realized I was an adult, I was a pro, I knew how to do comedy."

Rickles says of the Roast in his honor: "In those days the Friars Club was not so much a challenge between each other but just a big party. Today it's very competitive, and it's more or less, 'Watch my act and I'll watch your act. Let's hope I do good and you do good.' But my time at the Friars, when I had the Roasts, it was more of a party, in my opinion, than what it is today."

When Rickles was presented with a television at his Roast, he said, "I want to thank the Friars for

Jack Benny, Carl Timin, Joan Crawford, (and Joe E. Lewis) at the Friars dinner in honor of Ed Sullivan — 1968

giving me my tenth portable TV set. All of which, when you plug them in, they blow up. It was a very cheap gift." But of course, as with everything at these events, his comments were in jest. Today, Rickles says, "The Friars were very kind to me. Any presentation was always nice. If I said cheap, it's my humor, and I certainly would not say the Friars would give me a cheap gift. I don't think they would give anyone a cheap gift." And do guests of honor ever get angry and hold grudges? Not the ones who make a living out of doling out barbs, Rickles says. "Johnny Carson was a master at giving me ribs, and Mr. Sinatra every once in a while would take

Barbra Streisand got a little help from her friends Cy Coleman, Burton Lane, Harold Arlen, Jule Styne, Jerry Herman, and Harold Rome at her Friars Club testimonial dinner—1969

a shot at me. But it was always fun when they picked on me because they were great pros."

MUSICAL TRIBUTES

Barbra Streisand's 1969 dinner was certainly unique. It featured the top songwriters of all time performing parodies in Barbra's honor. Richard Rodgers, Jule Styne, Cy Coleman, Harold Arlen, Burton Lane, Harold Rome, and Jerry Herman "ivoried and sang humorous tributes to Miss Streisand," as *Variety* put it. A couple of the songs had to do with the situation surrounding the film *Hello, Dolly!* The movie's release was being held, awaiting a settlement with the show's producer, David Merrick. He was present on the dais, but he took the jokes in stride.

The songs weren't the only arrangements that were outstanding that evening, as *Variety* reported: "There was a bank of flowers that would have done credit to a Prohibition funeral."

Of course, humor played a big role too. Rodney Dangerfield was on hand to share his observations on how to be a hit in the mountains: "Just sing anything from *Fiddler on the Roof.*" Gene Baylos and Flip Wilson also joked for the folks, as did Joe E. Lewis, who quipped, "Nice to have you, B.S." Just in case the audience wasn't fully up to speed or was perhaps too far ahead, he did clarify that B.S. stood for Barbra Streisand.

Don Rickles went where no man had gone before, announcing, "Barbra, I want to say this publicly and from my heart: I never liked you!" She laughed just as hard as David Merrick had when he found the barbs bouncing all around him. Even her mother laughed when Rickles went on to say: "This Jewish girl, her mother a year ago was in Rockaway holding onto the ropes. . . . Your daughter's a dummy, Mom, I'll tell you that right now. You got a dummy daughter that made it and everyone is *shmeichel* her now." (Just in case your Yiddish is a little rusty, "*shmeichel*" means to "butter up.")

Flip Wilson, Robert Merrill, Ed Sullivan, and Rodney Dangerfield toast Barbra Streisand at her Friars Club testimonial—1969

Rickles still remembers that night fondly: "Barbra Streisand is a major, major lady in the biz. In fact, I'm on her anniversary disk," he says. "The audience enjoyed it, and I enjoyed saying it. I was very flattered that I was part of Barbra's life and to be able to rib her mother in good-natured fun."

Streisand also poked fun at herself, stopping the orchestra in the middle of a passage and asking if she was getting the "Entertainer of the Year" award all by herself. This was a reference to her sharing her first Academy Award with Katharine Hepburn. Streisand then sang "People" with special lyrics to mark her Friars occasion.

"My experience with the Friars Club was wonderful," Streisand recalls. "I'm sure much of that is due to the fact that it was a testimonial dinner as opposed to their famous Roasts, so it was a gentler approach. Seven American songwriters paid tribute to me through specially written lyrics to some of their greatest works. I can't tell you how incredibly touching that was to me. But the evening wasn't all about the music. I guess when it comes to the Friars you always have laughs

thrown into the mix. I remember Don Rickles being absolutely hilarious. By the time he was finished, I suppose you could say that I was roasted after all. But he was very funny, making jokes to my mother about me—it was sweet that he included her that way. It is an evening that I will always remember with a smile."

Hips were moving—and potentially breaking—at the 1970 dinner in honor of Tom Jones. Milton Berle, the emcee, told jokes that ran the gamut from Hollywood quips—"I feel like Lana Turner's next husband. I know what I'm supposed to do, but how can I make it interesting?"—to political jabs referencing an end to the Vietnam War—"Put it on ABC and it'll only last thirteen weeks!"

Paul Anka opened, though the band was a tad slow for his taste, provoking him to ask, "You guys playing for a funeral?" Louis Armstrong sang "Hello, Dolly!" Norm Crosby double-talked, and Dick Shawn did an imitation of Jones gyrating on stage that had the original shaking with laughter. Pat Henry explained Jones's movements this way: "If he stands still he sounds like Connie Francis."

Joe E. Lewis, Danny Thomas, and Buddy Howe present Barbra Streisand with the Friars Oscar at her Friars Club testimonial—1969

Dick Shawn doing the Tom Jones gyrate at Jones's Friars Club dinner — 1970

Glen Campbell sang and also accompanied Joe E. Lewis in his own rendition of a boozy "My Way."

This Roast was a first for Pat Cooper, who remembers: "I went to a Tom Jones Roast many years ago. He was hot as a pistol then. I was on the dais. I don't think I was asked to get up—I was just in awe of the whole damn thing. Things were happening for me. I didn't know how to handle it. I was more like, 'My God.' Coming from where I came from to be in that situation was like I was anointed, for Christ's sake. Coming from no education and problems with the family and all that garbage—and then to survive that and be a part of something with

some of these guys that have big names—I was in awe. But I was lucky I could handle it. I didn't get nuts, I didn't get egotistical, and I listened."

Buddy Arnold did his thing on this dinner as he had for so many others, saying, "I was writing *The Jackie Gleason Show* down in Florida, but I still wrote the Friars show—only I couldn't get up to New York to do the rehearsing of the guys. So we rehearsed it on the telephone. My helper in New York would keep an open phone for an hour. He would rehearse them, and I would critique it. Then I would get the guys, they had a loud speaker, and I would talk to them on the phone. Funny,

funny bit."

Jones gave a great private concert for the audience, singing his hits "Delilah," "In Other Words," and "If I Ruled the World," bowing to tumultuous applause and screams.

THE KING OF THE FRIARS AND THE QUEEN OF COMEDY

Only the Friars Club can put Gene Baylos and Coretta King on the same dais and end up with one of its more splendid affairs. When the Friars toasted Alan King in 1971, he brought his eclectic cross-sampling of friends along for the ride. The evening benefited the Robert F. Kennedy Foundation and the Martin Luther King, Jr. Foundation.

"I had, at one dinner, seven potential presidential candidates sitting on the dais," King remembers. "Oh yeah, and all the Kennedy girls—Ethel and all the other girls. Oh, and Hubert Humphrey." David Frost was the toastmaster, and the guest list

boasted Jack Benny, George Jessel, John Glenn, Harry Belafonte, Johnny Carson, Art Carney, Dionne Warwick, Red Buttons, Sidney Lumet, and George Segal. Not to mention politicos New York City Mayor John Lindsay, Ted and Joan Kennedy, George McGovern, Pat Kennedy Lawford, Jean Kennedy Smith, and so many others.

But all did not go smoothly. As the time came for the final marching order into the ballroom to be made, the confusion mounted. Names were being called, but in the midst of all the noise and a host of photographers trying to get their subjects to pose, nobody could hear. "Mrs. King?" the lead marcher called, and Jeanette King (Alan King's wife) and Coretta King stood up. They didn't know who was to go first, so they both left hand-in-hand. Jean Kennedy Smith, one of the last in line, said, "I feel like I'm in a dance."

Once the dinner was finally underway, Pat Henry took the dais and began ribbing George

Alan King with some of the Kennedy clan: Ethel Kennedy, Jean Kennedy Smith, Pat Kennedy Lawford, and Joan Kennedy at his Friars dinner—1971

Above: *Milton Berle gets Louis Armstrong to purse those famous lips — 1970s*

Left: *Carol Burnett looking stunning in cream pie as thrown by Harvey Korman at her Friars Club dinner — 1973*

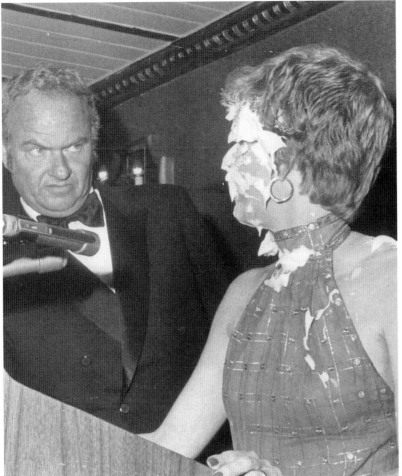

Jessel first, joking about getting high while sniffing the glue on Jessel's toupee and adding, "If Jessel's name isn't in the obit column, he calls up a dame." Henry then moved on to the guest of honor and applauded King for his civil rights work, saying that to follow King's example he would sometimes change places with his chauffeur while riding through Harlem in his Rolls Royce.

Alan was humbled by the accolades from the elite of entertainment and politics, saying, "I've never had this kind of an emotional experience before."

Carol Burnett was among the lucky Friars honorees; she only had to endure a testimonial dinner. Her 1973 fete was tamer than the Roasts, though

she did end up with a pie in her face at the end of it—thrown by Harvey Korman. It was all in fun, of course, and it was a fun time for everyone.

Freddie Roman remembers Burnett's dinner as his first official Friars Club event. "Carol was most gracious, and Dick Cavett was the emcee. Dick Cavett introduced me as one of the hot new comedians—that's how long ago that dinner was," Roman says. "My opening line got me right off the ground. I said, 'I'll never forget the first time I met Carol Burnett. It was during the salad.' And the place erupted and I was home free. Ed Sullivan was on the dais that night, and he walked over to me and said, 'Robert Klein, you're a funny man.' And he was serious. My wife and I looked at each other."

As for the queen of comedy, Carol recalls the evening this way: "I was thrilled when the Friars asked if they could honor me. I expected it to be

in England as he is here."

That evening, Milton Berle proved the Friars are the best when it comes to the domino theory of jokes—Youngman told a joke about Beame, so Berle told a joke about Youngman: "Henny Youngman has done for comedy what Ernest Borgnine did for tap dancing."

Matthau wore a black beret the entire evening, saying, "They shaved my head for *The Sunshine Boys* picture, and since I'm very vain, I won't be seen bald. My mother told me, 'Walter, don't you go out without something covering your head!'"

Alan King was the master of ceremonies, and he mentioned that Matthau's co-star, George Burns, was known for his generosity: "Any old broken-down actor can approach him, and he will open up his wallet—and show you a picture of his sister." After noting that Neil Simon's *The Sunshine Boys* was a play about a couple of feuding vaudevillians, King also said what was most likely on every Friar's mind that year: "That is real-

ly the story of the Friars."

A very special guest on the dais that evening was ninety-one-year-old Joe Smith, of Smith & Dale, the original Sunshine Boys. Smith performed both ends of an old Smith & Dale routine, including this snappy dialogue:

"I live by my wits."

"You live by your wits?"

"Yea, my Uncle Markowitz and my Aunt Berkowitz."

"How's business?"

"How should it be?"

"I'm glad to hear it."

"If you ever get to Florida, look me up."

"Where will you be?"

"In California."

FATHER AND SON AT THE FRIARS

Kirk Douglas was honored in 1977 with a testimonial dinner, and his good friend Gregory Peck was the emcee. Peck is not a comedian by trade, but he handled the humor flawlessly. He mentioned how the Breen office would not allow close-ups of Kirk's X-rated chin.

Douglas had an eclectic roster of speakers, performers, and guests. Lily Tomlin popped in between performances from a Broadway show. Paul Williams performed "Evergreen," the Oscar-winning song he wrote with Barbra Streisand, from *A Star Is Born*. Williams joked that the reason he was invited was, "They had to have somebody shorter than the mayor." Poor Abe Beame—it never ended.

The event even featured a telegram from Henry Kissinger, who couldn't attend. His absence left him open to ribbing, though, and George Segal stepped in with his take on

Milton Berle, Joe Smith (of Smith & Dale), Joey Adams, and George Jessel have some quiet time before getting down to the business at hand— roasting Joey—1976

Kissinger's movie-going status: "He's only missed two pictures in the last three years. He wouldn't go to see *All the President's Men* because he was afraid he'd recognize *Deep Throat*, and he wouldn't go to see *Deep Throat* because he was afraid he'd recognize *All the President's Men*."

Burt Lancaster then stepped up to the microphone, saying, "I was under the impression that anything to do with the Friars had to be a Roast. So I sat down at my desk and began to list things about my friend Kirk that were susceptible to ridicule." He then went on to explain that he had to nix anything he came up with for various reasons, so he called David Tebet, the producer of the event, to see about securing a writer. He said Tebet told him the dinner was a testimonial, not a Roast, so not to worry. That made for a very sweet evening for Kirk Douglas, but the rest of the audience missed out on the opportunity to hear Lancaster destroy his friend's ego.

"I'm a Friars baby," said Barbara Walters, who would have her own dinner in a decade or two. "I was brought up a Friar's child. My father is a man named Lou Walters, who had a marvelous nightclub called The Latin Quarter. I hate to think of the symbolism—it's now a porno flick place. My father had two clubs that he revered: one was the nightclub, the Latin Quarter, and the other was the Friars Club. The Friars was Dad's recreation. It was his home away from home. But he was so proud of being a member and so happy to be one. I think that I could support myself with no help from either NBC or ABC, with just the money that Dad lost in cards to Chico Marx."

Sammy Cahn wrote a parody for the occasion, to the tune of "There's No Business Like Show Business":

Songwriters saluting songwriters as Sammy Cahn is honored with a testimonial by Mitchel Parish — 1975

There's no Douglas like this Douglas
There's no Douglas like Kirk
Yes, I know the swell Helen Gahagan
And the great Supreme Court's William O.
I admit it's sacrilege and it is pagan
But if you're willing to lose some dough

There's no Douglas, like Kirk Douglas
Who does his kind of work
There is not a role that he has not portrayed
Not a part that he hasn't played
Though he never made the hit that Michael made
There's no Douglas like Kirk!

Successful son Michael spoke lovingly about his dad: "I've been looking forward to this for a long time—a tribute to my father. Which I knew had to have some semblance of a Roast. What better way for a son to vent his aggressions than through the guise of humor?" Too bad Michael's comedy writer fell ill, though, and he ended up saying some really nice things instead, though he did note that most of the accolades that evening were "much too pos-

Hats on to George Jessel, Henny Youngman, and Howard Cosell at the Friars Club's Roast in honor of George Raft — 1974

Milton Berle and Gene Baylos search for a punch line at the Friars Howard Cosell Roast — 1973

Redd Foxx has had enough laughs from Henny Youngman's firestorm delivery at Redd's Roast — 1975

Buddy Howe, Penny Marshall, and Burt Reynolds at the Friars Club's newscasters testimonial dinner honoring David Brinkley, Walter Cronkite, and Howard K. Smith — 1978

Elliot Gould writes down the good dirty jokes while Telly Savalas tells him how to spell the words that begin with "F" at the Friars Tom Jones Roast — 1977

itive, much too warm." He closed with, "You did a hell of a job bringing me up, and I hope your percentage in *Cuckoo's Nest* has us even."

Kirk was gracious in his comments: "Ladies and gentlemen, distinguished guests, this is not a Roast. This dinner is an annual tradition with the Friars, and it's always a big occasion, 'cause it's the only time the Friars get to see their wives. I'm especially proud tonight to be sitting on the same dais with my son Michael, the Oscar-winning producer. But you know, there have been a lot of malicious rumors about nepotism in Hollywood, and I want to set the record straight. I got where I am on my own, without any help from him.

"An identity crisis happened right in my home. My son Peter was watching a television show and I stood behind his chair to see what he was watching. He was watching Frank Gorshin doing an imitation of me talking to Burt Lancaster. You know, it's an uncanny imitation. It always amazes me, and as he was doing it I kind of kept watching and I tried to imitate Frank Gorshin doing me. As I was doing that my son Peter turned around and said, 'Dad, he can do you better than you can.'"

JOHNNY AND LUCY

"Johnny Carson, the patron saint of insomniacs," joked Toastmaster Bob Hope at the Friars testimonial dinner in honor of the king of late-night television in 1979. "This is an annual gig where the Friars honor someone as man of the year. And what do the Friars look for in an honoree? He must be of such stature and self-assurance and graciousness as to accept the barbs directed at him as an actual tribute from lesser people. Unfortunately, someone like that isn't always available. Then, in a typical act of charity, the Friars look for a prominent show-business personality in

Johnny Carson roasts his famous sidekick Ed McMahon — 1972

great need of adulation, love, and acceptance from his peers. Someone whose insecurity cries out for help. They use an evening like this to bolster his ego by making him the center of the attention he so strongly craves. Usually a man like this is available. Ladies and gentlemen, Johnny Carson needs lots of love."

The dais was composed of such personalities as Kirk Douglas, Barbara Walters, Mike Wallace, Suzanne Pleshette, Garson Kanin, Marvin Hamlisch, Jack Valenti, Ed McMahon, Doc Severinson, and many more. Some spoke, some just looked pretty, and all of them had a blast. Hope's jokes kept coming: "Johnny has a terrific contract with NBC—if he dies, they bury Rich Little. . . . Doesn't he look great? C'mon let's be honest, he's fifty-four and he looks it. . . . When he came into the world everybody had to move down one on the couch. . . . Johnny was born in Nebraska the year of the crop failure. His father said, 'I don't know whether I should have plowed deeper or used more fertilizer.'"

Lucille Ball was on hand to say a few words to

Lucille Ball looks up to Kirk Douglas at the Johnny Carson testimonial dinner—1979

Johnny Carson during his night as honoree. "Seventeen years ago, two great guys came into my life, simultaneously, and changed my sleeping habits," she said. "One was you, John, and the other, Gary Morton. Now, I admire you both, but naturally for different reasons. I've lost a lot of sleep because of you, Carson, but I've found a wild and crazy guy with Morton." Who says a lady can't have a little fun?

When Hope returned to the podium, he said, "In four movies Lucy played my wife, and we did passionate love scenes. Then at night she went home to her real husband. It's the story of my life—I gas up

the car, and someone else goes for the joy ride."

Lucille Ball took it all in stride—she was a very special Friars treasure who had been honored with a Roast of her own in 1961. And Carson had led that event in her honor. Cy Coleman, who composed the music for her Broadway show *Wildcat*, also was on the dais. "My very first Friars Club event was the Lucille Ball Roast," Coleman says. "Johnny Carson was the emcee, and he was just great. He said there were a couple of things the comics needed to steer clear of—one was her recent divorce to Desi and the other was to refrain from any foul language. He insisted that because she was a lady that he would

Robert Klein and Lucie Arnaz sing a duet from their hit Broadway show, They're Playing Our Song, *at the Friars Club testimonial dinner honoring Johnny Carson—1979*

keep the Roast clean and then introduced her as 'Lucille Testicle.' It was hilarious."

Lucy also had been honored by the Friars Club of California, along with Desi Arnaz. That dinner became memorable on both coasts when comedian Harry Einstein, known as "Parkyakarkus," died on the dais right after his turn as speaker. As Lucie Arnaz explains, "My first memory of the Friars Club is my mother telling me that Parkyakarkus died on the dais when she was being honored—isn't that a great memory? The first time I ever heard that there was a thing called the Friars Club.

I was a Catholic, and I thought they were a bunch of priests who walked around in long robes. So I said, 'Okay, so you went to a church and a man died on the dais.' I didn't know what a dais was, and his name was Parkyakarkus, so it's all bizarre. I thought she was talking Chinese."

Nearly two decades after that "bizarre" evening, Lucie joined her mother at the Carson dinner. At the time Lucie was co-starring on Broadway with Robert Klein in *They're Playing Our Song*. The pair entertained the crowd, with Marvin Hamlisch accompanying on the piano, playing the songs he had penned for that show. After finishing, Lucie Arnaz said, "I would really like to thank the Friars for allowing me to bring my mother with me."

When asked about the evening more than twenty years later, Arnaz apologizes for her memory loss. "I do remember performing with Robert outside of the show for a couple of big things, and we did it several different times. So other than saying I did it, I don't remember a thing about it. Not a damn thing." Thankfully, the recording of the evening keeps the memory of their dynamic performance going strong.

The Fifth Dimension, Hal Linden, and Robert Merrill also performed for Johnny, and Mike Wallace and the ambassadors to both Israel and Egypt were among the evening's speakers. Ruth Gordon told a very sweet joke that culminated in this little old lady belting out "bullshit!" several times, which had the audience laughing so hard they were in tears.

When Johnny finally stepped up to the microphone, he was classic Carson, saying, "So far, from where I have been sitting this has been a wonderful evening. And I thank all of the people on the dais and all of the performers. Ladies and gentlemen, Mr. and Mrs. Lincoln, it's been a wonderful show. The evening is running a little long. I should mention when Ruth Gordon arrived here tonight she was jailbait. Ruth, I must say, that was a fucking good speech.

"As you all know by now this is the seventy-fifth anniversary of the Friars Club. Coincidentally, sev-

Bob Hope greets Marvin Hamlisch at the Friars dinner in honor of Johnny Carson — 1979

enty-five years ago on this date the Friars had their very first "Man of the Year" dinner, and the guest of honor was George M. Cohan. And Bob, I understand you did a terrific job emceeing that, also.

"Doing an interview with Mike Wallace, or, as he is called all over the world, 'Mr. *60 Minutes*'— although I talked with his wife Lorraine last night and Lorraine told me you could diminish that by a factor of twenty. But having an interview with Mike Wallace is a special relationship in much the same sense that the village maidens had with the invading soldiers. Mike today, for example, just turned in his own mother for Medicare fraud.

"I could not be more honored or flattered that a gentleman who is truly an American institution would grace this dais tonight and serve as master of ceremonies, and Bob, I want to thank you."

Be it toasting, roasting, or frolicking, there is no denying the Friars know how to throw a party. While no one is spared their wit—charming, sardonic, or otherwise—everyone agrees that if you've been honored by the Friars you've made it. Ed McMahon is a member of that chosen few. "I was roasted several times," he says. "It's such an honor. You're honored by the worst things that anybody can say about you. It makes you feel wonderful. You're so blessed. You feel, what a lucky guy I am, these people saying these terrible things about me."

CHAPTER FIVE

FRIAR WITS AND JUICY BITS

The Mad Mad Mad Mad Events of the '80s and '90s

Opposite page: *Red Buttons,
Dick Cavett, and Joe Piscopo clown
around at Dean Martin's Friars
Club dinner — 1984*

W ith the Friars Club wit firmly in place, the "honor with jibe" tradition passed on by those bawdy founding fathers continues to echo throughout the hallowed halls of the monastery and beyond. While the jokes became even more stinging as the years went by, the honor continues to be revered.

As Norm Crosby will tell you, "There's an art to telling dirty stories, and that is what the good Friars—the good roasters— do. They use the dirty words, and they use the shock value as a tool, like an artist. They paint pictures with it, and it becomes wonderful when you utilize it that way. Being honored is a tribute—it really is. It's a great feeling, and even if they say terrible things about you, you know where they're coming from: 'We only roast the ones we love.' I believe that's true. I

really think that there's no finer tribute, when guys get together, when they make an effort, and they do their homework, and they have things to say about you, and they know a little bit about your background—it's a nice tribute. Even though you sit through the most vile things, you know where they're coming from and you know why they're there. And you just can't help but appreciate it."

Jerry Stiller, too, appreciates the value of these masters of comedy and their skills as verbal marksmen at their world-famous events. "Being at the Friars I never felt I really belonged, to be honest," he explains. "I always felt I was some kid who sat in the last row watching these great people that I adored. I was there as a student almost. These comedians had somehow or other mastered

the world in which if you spoke up everyone listened. And if you could say it in a funny way, that was the key to being somebody in this world.

"I still marvel at some of the things that I saw. Henny Youngman, at some Roast where he wasn't allowed to speak, suddenly he got up from the table and he walked over to the mike and he started talking. It was like being with your family when they get together for dinner. There are all kinds of torrents, all kinds of elements of a family—a lot of *gershrein*. There was so much rivalry, so much intrigue, so much stuff, that they started screaming at each other. You had no idea what it was, only that it was hilarious to watch them battling each other. I was very much in awe of all of this stuff."

Henry Kissinger seems like the last person the Friars would consider honoring; however, the club's history shows that heads of state are just as worthy as former classroom cut-ups. His 1980 dinner, with Kirk Douglas as master of ceremonies, was a class act. It included the following comment from the first lady of broadcast journalism, Barbara Walters, talking about his larger-than-life ego: "In the words of the immortal Henry Kissinger himself, who, looking around the room at another occasion when a group of dignitaries and celebri-

Henry Kissinger inspects his new watch presented by Buddy Howe at Kissinger's Friars Club testimonial dinner—1980

Rusty Staub and Milton Berle at the Friars dinner in honor of Buddy Hackett—1981

Freddie Roman and Jan Murray present Buddy Hackett with a watch at his Friars testimonial dinner—1981

ties gathered together to honor him said, 'I haven't seen this impressive a group since the last time I found myself in Versailles at the hall of mirrors.'"

Bob Hope always found that right mix of politics and humor: "I figure since this is an election year, you'd like to hear a comedian who isn't running for anything."

Speaking of politicians, Jacob Javits obviously hung around enough Friars Club testimonials to say, "I was present at a speech that Doc Kissinger made in the German Embassy, after he was Secretary of State. The room was very crowded and there were very few places to sit. So when Henry got to the lectern he looked around the room, as he does very deliberately, and he said, 'My friends, I apologize for the fact that obviously there are few places to sit, and I have a rather long speech but, you know, you can kneel.'"

In lieu of the "usual boring late-night speech" Kissinger threatened to read his book aloud, but somehow the audience was spared. However, in keeping with the portrait that the speakers painted of him this evening, he did comment, "The hour is late. As I take my seat I want to warn you that unless there is tumultuous applause, I will return to the podium and begin the reading of my book in

Jim Dale, Len Cariou, and Henry Youngman at Dale's Friars Roast — 1981

Frank Sinatra and Brooke Shields at Dean Martin's testimonial dinner — 1984

Dick Shawn thanks heaven he made it through his Roast to accept his watch from William B. Williams and Buddy Hackett — 1982

German." The room thundered with so much clapping, one would have thought a monsoon had hit the Waldorf Astoria. Was the applause for Henry or a way to escape the book reading? You do the math.

WOMEN AT THE FRIARS

It's pretty safe to say that when it comes to women being honored at the Friars Club, they can almost count on being in safe territory. And if you're Elizabeth Taylor, they'll definitely treat you with kid gloves. Dinah Shore was the mistress of ceremonies at Ms. Taylor's 1983 salute, and Dinah won a place in the Friars history book as the first woman to emcee a testimonial dinner. Sinatra stepped aside, Berle bowed, Carson tipped his hat, and, well, Jessel was dead, so the lady proudly sashayed up to the podium to run the show like the greats who had done so before her.

Dinah sang a parody of "Camelot" that Sammy Cahn wrote for the occasion:

> *She's always making headlines in the papers,*
> *keeps newsmen running till they're out of*
> *   breath.*
> *Sinatra even cannot match her capers.*
> *Elizabeth. Elizabeth. Elizabeth.*
> *Come let us hail a star of stars.*
> *Here's to Elizabeth. Elizabeth.*
> *Not England's, I mean ours.*
> *And so tonight we're here to greet a legend*
> *that I'm so pleased is in our favorite spot.*
> *And though the Friars are not exactly Camelot,*
> *tonight you will admit that they have got*
> *Elizabeth.*

At the same dinner, Ella Fitzgerald almost caused a riot when she mentioned out loud to the orchestra that she only had three minutes, and the

Elizabeth Taylor is Queen of her dinner with Dinah Shore as Lady in Waiting — 1983

song they rehearsed was longer. The crowd screamed and begged her to "sing what you rehearsed!" and damned if the lady didn't accommodate them. She belted out "Night and Day" and "Sophisticated Lady" and to hell with the timer!

When the Friars let Red Buttons loose on the dais, he surveyed the guests with a gimlet eye, though he, too, left the guest of honor alone: "Buddy Hackett, a man who makes pornographic records for the horny blind. My good friend Mr. Sinatra with us tonight, a man who has a gaming license in the state of Nevada to do anything he likes. My father was a tailor, but this is a wonderful woman. God bless you, Elizabeth."

Red also did a hilarious, "I Was There" routine, tailor-made for the Friars:

> *In Jerusalem at a wailing-wall rally to save the*
> *whales —*
> *I was there.*
> *In Saudi Arabia at an OPEC price-fixing*
> *meeting, not for oil, for hookers —*
> *I was there.*
> *In Greenwich Village, at a joyous gathering of*

Milton Berle, Lucille Ball, Angie Dickinson, and Red Buttons pal around at Dean Martin's testimonial dinner — 1984

*gay Hasidic stand-up comedians — I was
   there.*
*At the annual Beverly Hills High School 'guess
   who your father is?' PTA meeting — I was
   there.*

From "I Was There" to "Never Got a Dinner"
Red made it a two-for-one night of laughs:

*Gandhi's mother, who said to Mahatma, eat a
   cookie, whose gonna know?*
never got a dinner.
*King Henry the Eighth, who said to his lawyer
   forget the alimony, I got a better idea,*
never got a dinner.
Abe Lincoln, who said, a house divided is

a condominium,
never got a dinner.
*Moses, who said to the children of Israel, stop
   calling me Charlton,*
never got a dinner.
*Jesus, who never got a dinner, so they gave him
   a supper,*
never got a dinner.
*Santa Claus's mother, who said, since he got in
   the toy business he's never home for
   Chanukah,*
never got a dinner.
*Rex Harrison's doctor, who said to Rex, by
   George, I think you've got it,*
never got a dinner.

Cary Grant, Bernard Kamber, and Milton Berle reminisce about old times together at a Friars testimonial dinner — 1984

Dean Martin, Shirley MacLaine, Susan Lucci, and Sammy Davis, Jr. hang out together at Dino's testimonial dinner — 1984

Sinatra presented Taylor with a Piaget watch, calling her "our lady of the evening." Her reaction, not to mention the audience's, was very different from the one Mr. Sinatra surely must have expected. All in fun, of course. Ms. Taylor was ecstatic over the accolades heaped upon her by the singers and comedians, and she reveled in the audience's adulation. It was when she suggested the Friars elect a female abbot that the waiters started ducking for cover. Sinatra yelled, "This is a boy's club!" All in fun, of course.

Sometimes it can be a bit of a "sticky wicket" when the Friars honor women. A dinner is one thing, but a Roast? That's a bit different.

"The thing about the Friars is that they have a tribute," says Joy Behar, "and in the tribute, which I had, where my friends came and they talked a little about me, they were not really mean. That's always a lot more fun for the subject than being the object of the Roast, which could be a nightmare. You notice that they don't roast women much."

Joan Rivers agrees with Joy, and don't ask her if she'll be roasted: "Never! Never! Because I've heard all the jokes I want to hear. They're gonna be old jokes, they're gonna be plastic surgery jokes. Yeah, yeah, yeah—we've heard them. If they just said, 'Come, have a wonderful evening, it will all be funny, and everyone would all do their top five minutes,' oh, would I be there. A Roast? No. Oh yeah, here comes another plastic surgery joke. Ha ha ha."

"It's the lowest common denominator area that you can get a laugh with," says Susie Essman, weighing in on women being roasted. "It depends on who the roasters are. We did a tribute for Joy Behar, and it was all people who knew her. So there was tons of stuff for me, because she's one of my dearest friends. I have a million things I could roast about her without saying anything about what she looks like, as can most of her friends. So it depends on who you get as a roaster, I really think it does."

According to Behar, "Women are just a little

Frank Sinatra is flanked by Dionne Warwick and Barbara Sinatra at Barbara's testimonial dinner — 1988

more sensitive about their looks. I mean, you can call me a bitch, I don't really care. But if you say I'm fat, which I'm not anymore, big difference."

Behar, however, admits that there are a few women out there with some roast gumption: "Whoopi and Phyllis Diller. Phyllis Diller, you know, her whole act basically was all jokes about Fang, and whatnot. She's hilariously funny, but that was what her act was. So when they made

jokes about her looks, it was really a homage to her style. If they make jokes about how I look, it may not be so funny—to me. I remember when they took a crack at Richard Belzer's looks one time, and he was quite offended. I mean, nobody likes to have their looks made fun of."

When celebrities are asked if they would like to be roasted by the Friars, many look upon it as an honor. For one person, however, it was payback.

Phyllis Diller gets a ladies' watch from William B. Williams and Buddy Hackett at her Friars Club Roast. It was the Friars way of getting even with her for sneaking into a stag Roast two years earlier dressed as a man — 1985

"Phyllis Diller came to one dressed as a man," says Alan King. "Sat through the whole thing." She snuck into Sid Caesar's all-male Roast in 1983.

As Phyllis recalls, "All hell broke loose when a picture ran on the front page of the newspaper, and it showed me as a man. Everybody says I looked like Claude Rains!"

Her remark makes Jerry Stiller's comment about her even more telling: "To me she was one of the guys. A beautiful woman, who masked her soft side, but she was one of us."

Jack L. Green was one of the lucky witnesses to this historical moment: "I was there when she came in. She was wearing a grayish-blue suit. I didn't know it was a woman. She did it beautifully. And then, when it was exposed, of course there was a big laugh all around. It was after that they started talking seriously of letting women in. Before that I never remember women being involved. Even though we did roast Lucille Ball at one point, but she was the roastee rather than a guest in the audience."

Buddy Hackett was the roastmaster at Diller's celebrity luncheon and started things off as expected, calling it a "dickless luncheon." Although he did recommend the chicken croquets. "This is not the first time a lady has been honored," intoned Hackett. "Lucille Ball had a luncheon, but it was mixed. She had men and women present. And everyone was very goyish and talked with a small mouth and didn't say no bad words. We figured she had enough shit like that from Gary. Then we had one for Totie Fields, and that was all men, but it was subdued. People just tiptoed on one foot. But for Phyllis, it's all out, all out. Because last year she sneaked in dressed as a man, and she did the whole thing and then she told every newspaper she was here."

Younguns Richard Belzer, Gilbert Gottfried, and Jim Morris learning the roasting ropes at Ernest Borgnine's Roast — 1988

At the Roast, Jackie Vernon had some trouble with the microphone: "That's a switch, I can't get it down." Jack Carter labeled Ms. Diller, "Phyllis Dildo." Which prompted Phyllis to defend herself with, "Jack Carter has the disposition of an old Hoover vacuum cleaner—it sucks."

ROASTING IN THE '80s

In 1986 Jerry Lewis earned the status of roastee. He'd come a long way from his 1955 dinner, where Marilyn Monroe was the belle of the ball. "The French love him, they gave him the Legion of Honor, all's his hometown of Newark gave him was an enema," joked Roastmaster Buddy Hackett.

Alan King sized up the man by the caliber of his dais: "I have seen some great daises, but when I look up and down, it looks like the summer of 1940 at the Steel Pier." Howard Cosell wasn't too far behind in his assessment of both the dais and the guest of honor, "One by one they come and go, a bunch of decrepit relics of yesteryear each clinging to the same tawdry lines of the past worth nothing." Howard may have been an astute man,

Jack L. Green, Milton Berle, Bruce Willis, and Robert Saks show no hard feelings at the Bruce Willis Roast—1989

but did he have to be so honest all the time?

If Marilyn was the standout attraction at Lewis's first Friars event, Dick Shawn left a memorable impression at the second one. "One of my great, great recollections of a Roast," says Freddie Roman, "was Dick Shawn being introduced and getting up and pretending he was physically ill and spitting out, looking like he threw up. It was mushroom barley soup. I think that was the greatest single laugh I ever heard at a Roast. Sustained forever that laugh, and the people went nuts, it was out of this world. Absolutely insane. Completely off the wall. But he was that kind of a guy. He took chances. He was the last act; there was no way anyone could have followed that. Jerry wiped it off with a napkin. That was a highlight for me."

Jerry was presented with the Friars favorite gift, a Piaget watch. Jean-Pierre Trebot can't help but laugh anytime he's asked about the Lewis Roast. "You would think because I'm French he would have made my life easy, but no," Trebot explains. "At every event we do a mock presentation of the Friars Club gift to the guest of honor, as a photo op for the press. I handed Jerry his watch, and he threw it on the ground. I thought, 'Oh, he dropped it.' So I scooped it up, handed it to him and when the cameras started flashing, he threw it down again. This went on several times. He was laughing. During the actual Roast, when the dean at the time, Jackie Green, presented him with the watch formally, in front of the audience, Jerry said, 'Cheap piece of shit,' and laughed, saying, 'I threw it again, didn't I?' And damned if he didn't! He's a character, but he had a great time and it was a fun Roast."

If ever there was an odd coupling at the Friars it was Bruce Willis and Milton Berle at the Roast of Willis in 1989. (Okay, Milton Berle and Steven

Lauren Bacall, Ali MacGraw, and Marvin Scott at the Alan King testimonial dinner—1989

Seagal in 1995 was pretty over the top as well.) "Gentlemen, this afternoon is dedicated to the proposition that the continuous mention of the word 'fuck' will remind my prick of what it once used to do," said Berle in his capacity of roast-master. "Naming Bruce Willis the Man of the Year is like naming Dr. Ruth the fuck of the month."

This is probably the time to mention that this was the first Roast where Phyllis Diller could walk right through the front door, hair flowing and skirts billowing, if she wanted to. Women were now part of the audience. The stag Roast was officially a thing of the past, and Berle was ready to move into the twentieth century: "It is no secret for the first time we have ladies in our audience today. Welcome to you all. And don't any of you guys in the audience have any illusion about getting balled or laid. Not a chance, they're all Jewish housewives."

This was Stewie Stone's first working Roast.

Kevin Bacon and Paul Newman get to know each other at the Chevy Chase Roast—1990

"It was frightening," he says. "Milton was the emcee, and he was great, because if you would talk too fast he would pull on your pants saying, 'Slow down, slow down, slow down.' He would root for you, Milton, if he liked you. He rooted for you because Milton was the greatest with young comics. He'd say, 'Go for it, just go for it.'

"It was the first Roast they allowed women in, and I was nervous because you never know what to do. I had special material written for me. The worst thing you could do is have special material because you're the twenty-seventh guy to get up there, and everything you had written for you has

been said already. You're watching everyone on the dais cross out the jokes that they have. So when your time comes you have nothing left but, 'Oh hi, Bruce, nice to see you.'

"Now you're left with whatever you are as a human being, and if you're not used to it and if you don't trust yourself you're in the toilet. Every joke was taken, so I just said, 'There were these two guys....' I did some stock jokes and sat down. Because basically that's what works—your charm and a stock dirty joke. If you do cute things, they don't want to hear cute. They're not there to hear cute. They want to hear 'cocksucker,' 'motherfucker.'"

At the Chevy Chase Roast, Robin Leach, Sally Field, and Freddie Roman are all smiles, which is more than could be said about Chevy—1990

It was a huge dais with so many roasters that not everyone was able to get on. But it was not without its audio-visuals. Bruce Willis was presented with a watch, and then Bruce presented Uncle Miltie with a huge dildo. You either get it or you don't, so don't even ask.

As with Berle, every so often the Friars need to have a dinner for Alan King—just because. The one in 1989 was yet another historic moment, as Alan explains: "The second dinner, I had all my girls—Lena and Bacall. I ended up emceeing my own dinner. We couldn't get Carson, and I said,

'Hell, I'll do it.'" And he did.

"When I made the picture with Billy Crystal, *Memories of Me*," says Alan, "we'd be in the make-up room together. He would pump me for stories. I must have told him a million stories during the shooting of that picture, about the Friars and from vaudeville to nightclubs." So Billy was well versed in King's showbiz nostalgia. He was on the dais and mentioned that Alan was on *The Ed Sullivan Show* ninety-three times. For old-times sake he brought Ed back for Alan in a flawless imitation: "Alan, sorry I can't be there tonight, but I'm still dead." Billy then said of Alan during their time working together, "This is a man who can literally suck the oxygen out of a room. I had the bends for four weeks."

ROASTING RICHARD PRYOR

When the Friars roasted Richard Pryor in 1991, it wasn't all that clear if things would go off as planned. "We weren't sure from one moment to the next if Richard would be well enough by the time of the Roast," says Jean-Pierre Trebot. "Bob Saks, who produced that Roast, would make daily calls, getting updates on his health. With all of his health problems we had a very long summer wondering if we could pull this off in the fall." But they did, indeed, pull it off, and with Robin Williams as roastmaster it proved to be one of their most successful.

Pat Cooper pretty much expressed what Trebot was feeling all summer long: "The greatest line I think I ever threw is at Richard Pryor's Roast. I got up and said, 'When are you gonna die?' I said, 'Jesus Christ, you burn yourself, you smoke yourself, you needle yourself. Italians know how to die. We lay down, we die.' I said, 'Do me a favor, why don't you die tonight? You'll be a big hit.' They screamed." Pryor was indeed pounding the table at that point.

When David Hyde Pierce studied up on his roasting skills for Kelsey Grammer's Roast, he viewed some tapes of previous Friars Roasts, "It's very hard to draw lines in that circumstance, because part of the fun is crossing the line. I think it has more to do with the talent of the individual performer. You can tell when someone crosses a line just because they don't have a better way of getting a laugh versus someone who so artfully crosses a line. I remember a line about Pryor from Robin Williams: 'The man who proved that not only is black beautiful, it's flammable.' That was amazing that he went there, but it was a real artfully constructed joke."

Pierce also recalls, "Gene Wilder did one for Richard Pryor where he talked about how Richard was secretly in love with him, and it was so off the wall and so inspired."

Joan Rivers was in attendance at this Roast. "Oh, that was the most amazing thing I've ever been in," she recalls. "It was amazing because you saw the respect of the entire community. People flew in from all over. I've never seen a gathering like that on a dais. It was astonishing. If they had blown up the Hilton ballroom there would not have been one A comic left in the world. It was amazing, and what a tribute to him.

"I thought Robin Williams was wonderful. It was just such a sadness in that room because Richard

was comparatively young, and he was the first one of us, whatever 'us' means, to become ill. They wheeled him in; it was so astonishing and so awful because I think this was the most brilliant mind.

"I came late, and by the time they got to me, everyone had said everything. There were like twenty-odd people roasting. He had just been burned, and I know I had burn jokes, and then Robin Williams had burn jokes, so I crossed those out. Then I had divorce jokes, and somebody else had divorce jokes, so I crossed that out. So by the time it got to me I just said I loved him and adored him. But I did start with him in the beginning, in the Village, and I was just thrilled to be there with him."

Rivers brings up an occupational hazard among Friars at a Roast: "You work so hard on your material and I'm a slow worker. I mean, if I'm going to do something, I work five or six days before, honest. And really work on it and do drafts of it and all that stuff. Then you're sitting there and someone has the same topic and just about the same jokes and you go, 'Oh shit.' That's very frustrating. I've learned my lesson. Don't wait to be near the end. Get up in the beginning, do it and sit down and enjoy yourself."

Joy Behar agrees with Rivers: "Here's the trick to the Roast—you can't go on last. Because all the jokes have been done already. One of the keys to

being in the Roast is to start early. Of course, you can't always get that slot depending on what kind of clout you've got. Use your imagination, come up with something different. But, on the other hand, you're dealing with stereotypical personas here. They have their stage persona, which is what everybody knows."

Chevy Chase wished he, too, had gone on first when his time to roast Pryor came. While looking at Robin Williams he said, "Every joke I wanted to tell, you told. What a coincidence."

Bill Murray solved that problem altogether. He stood at the podium and said, "I'm not prepared to speak, does anybody have any questions?" And he meant it! He stood waiting for questions, but the crowd was too busy laughing at his deadpan manner to even come up with one. When he did speak it was in tribute to Pryor: "I think that Richard Pryor is the funniest damn comedian I've ever seen in my life." It was an amazing tribute to an amazing comedian.

MUSIC, BLACKFACE, AND PUPPETS

Every so often the Friars change gears and let the music take center stage. Of course, this means giving comedy the night off but sometimes it's worth it. In 1992 they honored Clive Davis with a testimonial dinner. The music mogul was the head

Scenes from the touching—and hilarious—Richard Pryor Roast in 1991: From left to right: *LL Cool J and David Carradine; David Dinkins gives the go-ahead to roast Richard; Chevy Chase, Robin Williams, Richard Pryor, and Quincy Jones; Anthony Quinn, Joan Rivers, Norm Crosby, and Brian Dennehy; old pals Richard Pryor and Gene Wilder*

of Arista Records at the time and the talent was, simply put—awesome. Aretha Franklin, Kenny G, Jennifer Holliday, Whitney Houston, Barry Manilow, and Dionne Warwick all performed for their boss. Dionne was flown in on a special plane after suffering back problems at the airport in LA—when Clive calls, people come.

For Susan Lucci this evening was a highlight. "It was all music and I thought, 'Wow, this is very exciting for me to be here.' It's before I started singing, so I was there purely by the seat of my pants." Along with Lucci on the dais there was Master of Ceremonies Roger Moore, Sammy Cahn, Frances Ford Coppola, Betty Comden, Adolph Green, Jerry Orbach, Brooke Shields, Jule Styne, and even Martha Stewart. According to Lucci: "I

like a ballerina with chorus boys. She was hysterical. It was so funny and showed such a great sense of humor on her part."

It's probably a safe bet that those original eleven press agents who founded the Friars Club are just a bit relieved they turned the club over to the entertainers, so they can wash their hands of what went down at Whoopi Goldberg's oh-so-infamous Roast in 1993. As you probably know, Ted Danson, as roastmaster, came out in blackface and caused one or two red faces. A photographer from the press happened to be in the ballroom and happened to take a photo that happened to wind up on the front page of the *New York Daily News*.

Joan Rivers devoted an entire segment of her television talk show to the incident: "I spoke out.

Clive Davis received a musical tribute in 1992. From left to right: *Whitney Houston and Bobby Brown enter the ballroom; David Tebet, Clive Davis, Roger Moore, and Jack L. Green pose for a photo; Aretha Franklin and Susan Lucci meet during the evening.*

remember a couple of things that stand out. I remember Cy Coleman going up and down the dais bumming cigarettes, which I found totally adorable. I don't smoke but I thought, God that's so charming. But what really knocked my socks off was Aretha Franklin performing. She sang 'Like a Natural Woman.' She had on a pink ballet-like tutu and ballet slippers. She sat at the piano, I believe, and played and sang and then got up and danced

I was so upset. First of all, it's funny. Let's all calm down. They're living together. He adores her. There's no disrespect here. And if it had been a black man putting on a white face, nobody would have said one word. I thought it was such a double standard. I thought it was so totally ridiculous. It's a man that's madly in love, and they're living together. Would you stop it? I just thought somebody should just speak out and say how stupid it

Muhammad Ali laughing at Billy Crystal, which happened over and over at Billy's Friars Club Roast — 1992

Freddie Roman, Jerry Orbach, and Buddy Hackett at the Roast in honor of Billy Crystal — 1992

George Kennedy, Norm Crosby, and Kevin Costner sit a spell before heading into the Hilton Hotel Ballroom for Billy Crystal's Roast — 1992

was. And he had to apologize? What the hell was this?" After that show aired, Rivers says, "My phone lines lit up, of course. You always have people screaming."

Ironically, Ted joked about the press even then: "The tabloids, they just won't let us alone. This morning Whoopi said to me, 'You know, if only we can get Burt Reynolds to fuck Michael Jackson maybe we'd be home free. Maybe they'd let us alone then. It's tough being in the tabloids." Famous last words.

"It just wasn't meant to be seen by the public," says Norm Crosby, who was on the dais that night. "It wasn't meant to be reviewed. It was a private, very personal, lock-the-door Friars affair. The minute they opened the door and let people in, it became absurd. Montel Williams walked off and called every newspaper and said it was like a lynching, it was like slavery. Whoopi thought it was sensational. Whoopi loved it. I said, 'Well, she loved it! What are you complaining about?'

"I don't understand any of that. It wasn't meant to be an open-door policy. We locked the doors. We told the waiters and waitresses to get out. Lock the doors. That's the way it should be."

Whoopi pretty much summed it up when she turned to Ted that afternoon while doing his thing at the podium and said, "Welcome to the dais, baby, We're in this together."

In 1994 the Friars roasted Bob Newhart with Don Rickles as roastmaster. "It's tough to make fun of you because you are a total bore," snapped Rickles. Newhart is a tough guest of honor because of his G-rated demeanor, as Norm Crosby pointed out that day. "The format for a Friars Roast is to find a guest of honor and then have people come up here and call him an 'asshole' and a 'schmuck' and a 'motherfucker,' and stuff like that. I cannot do that today to Bob Newhart because Bob does not fit that mold. Those words are not suitable nor applicable for Bob Newhart, I'm not comfortable with that. Now, if we were roasting Don Rickles then I have no problem."

Norm talked about how close Rickles and Newhart were and how they would travel together. One trip to Africa prompted this joke: "There was a missionary down there at the same time that they were having their safari. The guy took a walk

Donald Trump and Robin Williams caught in the act of having a good time at the Billy Crystal Roast — 1992

Odd Couple Tony Randall and Jack Klugman fit right in at the Friars Club's Neil Simon dinner— 1993

Kevin Spacey and Neil Simon get happy at Neil's Friars Club fete—1993

in the deep part of the jungle and he found himself surrounded by natives with spears and bones in their nose. Evil, vicious-looking guys and he looked up and he said, 'God, I'm fucked.' And a voice from the sky said, 'No, my son, I am with you, have faith. Grab the spear from the nearest native and stick it right into the chief.' And he grabbed the spear from the nearest native and he stuck it into the chief and the voice from heaven said, '*Now* you're fucked.'"

Crosby also talked about traveling with Don and Bob to Israel: "I remember going to the statue of the Israeli Unknown Soldier. It was a magnificent edifice, a big monument, and it said, 'Israeli Unknown Solider—Morris Finkelstein.' And I said to the guide, 'How can you call him an unknown soldier when you know his name?' And the guide said, 'Because as a soldier he was unknown, but as a furrier everybody knew Morris.'"

Larry, Darryl, and Darryl, the three hicks from *Newhart,* shared some real nasty—but funny— comments on the real backwoods Bob. Dick Martin started out his set with, "Bob is a eunuch. I mean unique."

Pat Cooper was on the dais that afternoon and gave the crowd a few of his best hits: "Phyllis Diller was supposed to be here but she's doing the centerfold for *Popular Mechanics*. I don't know Bob Newhart that well, the man's got three fuckin' series, he's a fuckin' bore. I'm a genius—I can't get radio.

"What burns my ass is Bob Saks said he was gonna bring me back every other year, so in other words, this year I'm here, next year I can't come and they're gonna roast Jesus Christ....Here's a guy, looks like a fuckin' tailor, he gets three series. I'm gonna end my career here, I don't give a shit. I want to be remembered for one thing—nothing.

"You're a classy man because you're a friend of Don Rickles. Why is Don your friend? Because

Robert Saks, Ted Danson, Robin Williams, Whoopi Goldberg, Michael Douglas, Robert De Niro, and Jack L. Green are ready to face an afternoon they will never forget at Goldberg's Friars Club Roast—1993

you're always sleeping, he keeps you awake." Well, not everybody gets every joke at these things so when the laughs didn't quite come after that one, Pat quipped, "I'll never say that again as long as I live." *That* one got a laugh.

Cooper closed with, "But at least I'll say one thing—Abe Beame, he talked to my crotch. A fuckin' mayor talked to my crotch, a fuckin' nobody." When Cooper left, Rickles said, "Thank you, Pat, you were just great as always. Just a relaxed little Italian guy. . .guy's gotta be sedated."

Susie Essman was at this Roast. "I grew up on

Don Rickles, watching him on Johnny Carson," she says. "I just thought he was the funniest person alive. So I was thrilled to go to that. It was the first Roast I was ever at, and I remember thinking this is really fucking hard to do. I don't know if I can ever do this." For the record, she not only can do them she became the second woman to emcee one, so she proved her Roast-mettle.

Mal Z. Lawrence closed the show: "We're honoring a man who's a role model for people with no personality, ladies and gentlemen. I have to roast Newhart, the same little horny schmuck I grew up with. I know when he took out his little pecker and he pulled it for the very first time. He smiled. I thought it was disgusting—he was using my hand." Looking down at Newhart to his left and Rickles to his right, Lawrence said, "I'm standing here between the comedy mask and the tragedy mask."

When Newhart got up to respond in kind to the many, shall we say, *accolades* he was given, he pulled out two puppets. That's right. One bore a frightening resemblance to Rickles and the other to Dr. Henry Kissinger. The comedian then did a ventriloquist act, complete with moving lips and his trademark stammering. Even Newhart must have realized how this was going over, remarking, "A better man would have quit by now, but I wrote this shit and I'm going to finish it!"

"I could have walked on water when I saw that," laughs Pat Cooper, remembering the puppets. "If I gotta go around and make dummies, I'll quit. I like the both of them and I think the both of them are great. I love Don and I love Bob Newhart and in fact I said, 'Bob, I got news for you, don't ever do this again.' And he started to laugh."

Rickles remembers the Roast fondly: "A close friend is sometimes a little more difficult because you know them so well and there are so many things you can say. The Bob Newhart Roast was the highlight of my life, and I had a good time doing it."

THE APPLAUSE AWARD

The Friars, however, are not just about hilarious Roasts of great comedians.

The Friars Foundation each year holds a dinner at the Plaza as a fundraiser for its charitable giving. They honor individuals with their coveted Applause Award, which is a far cry from the Friars Roast Award. They have honored the best and the brightest in entertainment, luminaries such as Abraham Beame, Tony Bennett, Frances Preston, Lionel Hampton, Leo Jaffe, Kander and Ebb, William B.

Carol Burnett charms Tony Bennett (or maybe it's the other way around) at the Friars Foundation dinner in honor of Tony Bennett—1994

Diane Sawyer, Louis Malle, and Candice Bergen chit chat at Barbara Walters's testimonial dinner—1994

Williams, Frank Military, Comden and Green, Cy Coleman, and Harry Belafonte, to name a few. Turning out to pay tribute to the guests of honor have been such names as Liza Minnelli, Donna Summer, Gloria Gaynor, Red Buttons, Jane Powell, Bobby Short, Robert Klein, Lucie Arnaz, Len Cariou, Jerry Orbach, Tony Roberts, James Naughton, Michael Feinstein, Eddie Fisher,

Maureen McGovern, Jule Stein, and so many more.

The Friars Foundation Dinner is a quiet, demure affair that often makes the society pages. When they honored Ted Turner in 1996, however, it made the gossip columns. "This is in happier days, when Jane and Teddy were together," recalls Joy Behar, who performed at the dinner. "It was very shortly thereafter that they split because, and

Carol Channing presents Barbara Walters and Henry Kissinger at Walters's Friars Club honor — 1994

I read this, that the reason he dumped her is because she found Jesus and he found a nineteen-year-old named Tiffany."

Maybe Ted and his then wife, Jane Fonda, weren't happy about their meal or maybe they didn't care for the design of the Applause Award. If the truth be told, it's not for everybody's mantel. The award has two bronze arms growing out of a base to form clapping hands, so in fairness to Ted and Jane, it may not have gone with their décor. In any case, when Master of Ceremonies Alan King was about to start the show and introduce the couple, they were

nowhere to be found. "It's like the Eddie Duchin story where Eddie disappears from the piano at the end of the movie and all of a sudden the piano is still playing and where's Eddie?" laughs Joy.

Alan's testimonial became an instant Roast, because that's what they do. "Fuck Ted Turner! And, Jane, you got a big ass!" When Julie Budd got up to sing, she gave the couple an out, commenting, "Maybe it was the chicken." So what happened to the "tribute"? "Behind their back, people just turned on them," says Behar. Let this be a warning to any future honorees. Stick around for the show.

Bob Newhart and Don Rickles with Newhart's Roast Award — 1994

Friars Foundation Chairman Leo Greenland, Ted Turner, Friars Foundation President Cy Leslie, Alan King, and Jane Fonda before things went south at the Friars Foundation's Applause Award in honor of Ted Turner — 1996

Freddie Roman, Frances Preston, Donna Summer, and Louise DuArt celebrate Preston's Friars Foundation Applause Award — 1993

CHAPTER SIX

THE JOKES STILL FLY AS THE EGOS DIE

Recent Years of Roasting and Toasting

Over a hundred-year period, there are bound to be a few stand-out moments that push the story-tellers into overdrive with their "Did you hear the one about ...?" tales. We've already touched on many of them. Jimmy Durante arrested on a Friars dais; Mike Todd's untimely death on his way to his Friars dinner; Phyllis Diller's uninvited transgendered moment; Ted Danson's politically incorrect makeup—not an endless list but a unique one. Kelsey Grammer's Roast surely deserves such an honored place in the Friars scrapbook. The day before his 1996 Roast he flipped his Dodge Viper and entered the Betty Ford Clinic.

"I was sitting in the dining room having lunch with Jean-Pierre Trebot," says Norm Crosby. "I had come in from LA for the Roast, and I was looking at the menu. I thought I'd have

a roast beef sandwich. Somebody came over to the table and said to Jean-Pierre, 'The Roast is cancelled.' So, I looked up at the waiter and said, 'Well, then I'll have the chicken.' I thought he meant the roast beef was cancelled! They were hysterical. And nobody realized what he was saying. He said, 'Kelsey had an accident with his car and we had to cancel the Roast.'"

The Roast did go on, two months later. Sally Jessy Raphael points out an apparent Friars requirement: "It's amazing how many people come to us directly from the Betty Ford Center. It's almost a prerequisite—after you've been to Betty Ford, come and see us."

David Hyde Pierce was the roastmaster, and he said if Grammer agreed to go through with it then

David Hyde Pierce is caught in the act of roasting Kelsey Grammer — 1996

they would not hold back. The club decided to wait for two months, when Kelsey got out of rehab. "Good afternoon, fellow students of the Friars Club traffic school," said Pierce. "This is what happens when you let things fester for a couple of months. I'm proud to present this award to Kelsey Grammer. I must apologize, I've gotten no sleep. I keep getting calls from the woman Kelsey knocked up at the Betty Ford Center, and I keep telling her, 'Betty, go home, there's nothing for you here.'"

Norm Crosby gives two thumbs up to Pierce's roastmastering skills. "David Hyde Pierce had never done it before, and he did a great job," says Crosby. Pierce admits he had some talented help: "You are so blown away by just the regular stand-ups who are so good at what they do. I knew I needed a good writer because I knew it wasn't my territory. That's when I called Bruce Villanche, who I had met doing other things. He was at award shows where I was a presenter, so I had a mini-taste of what it was like to be a host and what it was like to work for Bruce and how good he was. He's amazing because he can write as much or as little as you need. If you are in serious trouble, he can write your whole act for you. If you can do stuff on your own, you can take him as a launching pad. What I ended up doing was a real mix."

Jane Leeves and Peri Gilpin—Kelsey's co-stars on *Frasier*—also bravely roasted their boss: "We've decided to bring Kelsey a few little items we feel he may need. First on the list is a dick warmer." The girls pulled out a frightfully large sock, then said, "Wait a minute, that's David's. Oh, here." Needless to say, the tiniest sock was then pulled out of their bag of tricks. "A watch, a pair of handcuffs, you know, he's probably already got those— he's been jailed many times. He has a rap sheet as long as David's dick warmer."

Sally Jessy Raphael, Kelsey Grammer, and Damille Donatacci Grammer right before Kelsey was led to the slaughter — 1996

After actress Hazelle Goodman's rapid-fire roast, the audience, and Kelsey, didn't know what hit them: "What better place to talk about my new book, *Jungle Frasier, My Secret Love Affair with Kelsey Grammer*. . . . I got a telegram from Ted Kennedy, he says, Congratulations on today's honor. Can he get a ride over to the clinic after the Roast?. . . When it comes to oral sex let's just say that he has bad Grammer. . . . David's hide ain't the only thing that's pierced. . . . I'm suing Kelsey for support of our secret love child—Urkel." Goodman also harkened back to Whoopi Goldberg's Roast: "Montel, are you in here? You don't have to walk

out on me. This black face doesn't come off."

This was Sally Jessy Raphael's first Roast, and she recalls, "Nobody told me that they used a lot of four-letter words. I wasn't expecting it. I don't find it particularly funny. I find it a replacement for being funny, which is a different ballgame. It was pretty shocking. Today, of course, nothing shocks, so we've done away with it. To people who come to the Roast, expecting a lot of shocking phrases, I would not know what to do that's shocking. I don't think there is anything shocking. It's all been done, so we've cleaned our act up."

This was a very different role for Pierce, the

David Hyde Pierce shares a laugh with Phyllis Diller at the Kelsey Grammer Roast—1996

gifted thespian. "The only perception people had of me was playing Niles on *Frasier*, and they didn't know what they were in for," he says. "I think that Bruce's genius there was to say that you were in for exactly what you always get and maybe even a little bit more. I thought it was pretty down and dirty what I got to say, and I had a great time."

Of all the Friars Roasts, Grammer's ran a very fine line between entertainment and verbally beating a man when he's down. Pierce was well aware of the delicate path this event was treading upon: "Those were serious problems. He had been in ter-

rible trouble, and in a way he may have been a better candidate or an easier candidate before all that, before he had really hit bottom. But on the other hand, it was his strength coming out of all that, and his resolve and his ability to say, 'Enough is enough, I'm going to clean my life up.' That gave us all the okay to nail him. I didn't run anything by him. I am sure at some point I said to him, 'I'm gonna really do this,' and he knew and expected me to. It was that Kelsey had really landed on his feet and was okay, and this was like cauterizing the wound, almost."

It would be a disappointment if Jeffrey Ross ever held back: "What can I say about Kelsey Grammer that hasn't already been said on *Hard Copy*? Kelsey would have brought his girlfriend here tonight, but she has detention. Kelsey's movie *Down Periscope*, I wanted to see it in the theater but I was busy that day. I heard Siskel and Ebert gave it two thumbs up their asses."

NBC Entertainment President Warren Littlefield also got into the comedy act: "All those years of playing a psychiatrist on television has really taught him one thing—how to fake a prescription."

Appearing for the first time at such an important Friars venue was not lost on Pierce: "I wasn't ever nervous about going into disgusting areas or being dark or blue or rude, but doing it in front of all these people who do it for a living, that's the scary part. I didn't want to be accepted as a charity case. I didn't want people to say, 'Well, for an actor, he did a pretty good job.' I wanted to do a good job. I wanted for people to genuinely laugh and have a good time and feel like this was a real Roast." Oh, it was more real than many that had gone before.

TOASTING TRAVOLTA

Hollywood came to the Friars in 1997 when they saluted John Travolta and Kelly Preston with a testimonial dinner with Larry King as the master of ceremonies. Lauren Bacall, Harry Belafonte, Nora Ephron, Louis Gossett, Jr., Mariel Hemingway, Anthony Hopkins, Lauren Hutton, Harvey Keitel, Sally Kellerman, Arnold and Anne Kopeslon, Shirley MacLaine, Mace Neufeld, Eric Roberts,

Kyra Sedgwick, Sylvester Stallone, Harvey Weinstein, Debra Winger, and Sean Young all showed up to air-kiss the Travoltas.

"I remember the turnout was so awesome because it was all these wonderful artists that came. It was a big deal," says Travolta of the evening. He was humbled by the dais of shining stars as well as by Anthony Hopkins. The two stars had never met before, but over cocktails Hopkins told Travolta that he was there solely because he admired the guest of honor's work. Travolta recalls, "That was probably what moved me the most, was that comment. Anthony Hopkins was at the pinna-

John Travolta and Kelly Preston meet Anthony Hopkins for the very first time at their testimonial dinner—1997

cle of his career, and for him to say that and actually show up really impressed me. I was taken back by that in a wonderful way. When you don't expect to be admired and then someone surprisingly does, you feel humbled by it to some degree."

As with most savvy celebrities, when it comes to the Friars they need to do their homework before accepting any honor. "I was surprised at first because I didn't know there were two kinds of evenings," says Travolta. "There's the kind where you actually get fried, and the other kind where they honor you. I said, 'Well, I'm really not up for being made fun of all night, so what do you want to do with me?' They said, 'No, no, no, this is another kind of night. This is an honor.' So I said, 'You mean no one makes fun of me? Wow, if I'm going to be honored and not made fun of, then I'll come.'"

The entertainment was a mixture of music and comedy. How's this for an odd pairing: The Friars Club and the Village People? They performed their

Sylvester Stallone gets into a deep discussion with Shirley MacLaine—either that or she mistook him for a waiter and wants another Pepsi at the Travolta dinner—1997

hit "YMCA." Enough said. The Bee Gees were also there to talk about John's *Saturday Night Fever* days. They didn't plan on singing but did do an a cappella version of "How Deep Is Your Love."

Joy Behar told the happy couple they were lucky to have been married for six years at that point and suggested that Kelly hold onto John. "It's very hard to find a guy, especially if you're a woman over a certain age," she advised. "You know, they say that the chances of a woman getting married after forty are equal to being kidnapped by terrorists, did you know that? Fortunately for me these two things are equal, although with a terrorist there's a chance of getting laid once in a while. There I said it! A cute guy in a turban, what's so bad?"

Harvey Keitel and Sean Young enjoy each other's company at the Travolta dinner—1997

Jeffrey Ross recalls the event: "One of my first big nights as a Friar wasn't a celebrity Roast but a toast for a dinner honoring John Travolta and his wife, Kelly Preston. It was very exciting. Another comic on the show was Ray Romano. I don't think either of us had ever performed in a tuxedo before. A lot of big stars were there. My childhood hero, Sylvester Stallone, spoke right before me, then I got up and said, 'This isn't a big night for them— this is a big night for me! Next week I'm at the Holiday Inn in Nyack!'"

Ray Romano, tux and all, was honored to be there: "This is kind of nerve-wracking. I'm not a Friar. This is the closest I've been to a Friar event. I mean, my father took me to a Christmas party at the Elks once, that's as close as I got. I don't know if there's an affiliation."

One never knows at these events just when that fine line between Roast and toast will be crossed. Alan King started in on the couple by noting that they didn't seem to have many black friends on the dais, but he quickly set the record straight, as did Harry Belafonte, who related both Travolta's and King's fostering of civil rights. But, hey, you just never know, do you, John?

"I think that with Alan King, it was like, oh my goodness, where are we going?" Travolta says. "But really, it was usually immediately modified. I also just got the idea that because of the people like Larry King and others that were there, it just wasn't going to go in that direction. So, I appreciated that, too."

Ending the show, John and Kelly turned their speech into a song parody that brought the house down. Travolta remembers: "I think it came out of a desperate move to make it go right. I take pride in whenever I have to accept or do an acceptance

Kelly Preston and John Travolta sing the Friars praises: "Tonight we were laughers and criers, we ended up Friars!"—1997

speech. I felt that in this case, something entertaining was more apropos. The singing and dancing thing I felt would be a kind of spoof on ourselves. We had the luxury of not being roasted, so I thought, well then, we kind of can roast ourselves and make fun of ourselves a little bit. And that would be an appropriate thing."

Travolta still remembers what went through his head as he held his Friars Club Oscar: "I was thinking, this is a really good time, a good night, and a memorable one."

THE FIRST ROASTMISTRESS

Joy Behar entered the Friars record book in 1997 by becoming the first female roastmaster, or as the Friars prefer, roastmistress. One might think that Dinah Shore held that distinction for emceeing Elizabeth Taylor's dinner, but there is a huge difference between overseeing the dinners and the Roasts. "Somebody asked me about it, and I said, 'Well, yes, I am the first in the history and welcome to the sixteenth century,'" Joy says.

"That's why, when I stepped up to the podium

and I let loose with some very weird language, I got a laugh right away because they felt comfortable." Behar had no hesitation when she was asked to helm the Friars' most sacred of events: "I did want to do it, because it was historical for the Friars, and I liked being the first woman. I thought that was an honor. And also because I thought that Danny Aiello was a great target. I immediately had visions of material. Which is very important when you do a Roast."

Before the Roast, Richard Belzer commented, "We're taking no prisoners. He's going down for the count. There's no other way. It's a Friars Roast, you can't hold back." And he didn't. One of the highlights of the Roast was Belzer's reading several unfavorable reviews of Aiello's short-lived television series, *Dellaventura.*

Pat Cooper roasts Danny Aiello — 1997

According to Joy: "That's all he had to do to Danny. It destroyed him! The man cried. According to Danny, he hadn't even seen them. This was the first time he had heard them. Then he started to talk about his mother and, of course, he broke into tears at that also, because he's Italian. Hello? I told that to Belzer when I saw him. I said, 'You made a guy cry. He really was upset.' 'Who cares?' he said. Belzer couldn't give a hey."

When Belzer finished reading the horrible reviews, he said, "I've known Danny for twenty-five years, we'll see if it continues." Everyone there that day is wondering the same thing. Joy's comment at the Roast about Danny's show was, "*Dellaventura* is the Italian word for thirteen weeks."

Bring up the Aiello Roast to Susie Essman and

she'll finish the sentence for you: "And then Danny cried. That's what's memorable to all of us. That's the one where Joy was the first female roastmistress and there hadn't been another one since, 'til I did the Smothers Brothers. I hope that somebody else comes after us though."

This Roast was a milestone for Essman as well. "The Danny Aiello Roast was the first Roast I ever performed at," she says. "That was interesting because nobody wanted me on that Roast. They just thought, 'Who's this little girl?' I remember Kenny Greengrass, who was producing it, calling me up and telling me he was going to put me on. I'm thinking, 'I gotta do this. I know that I know how to do this.' I remember that Roast very, very well because that was a big deal for me, to do that Roast. I'm always a nervous wreck until I get onstage and then

Jeffrey Ross with his favorite Roast topic, Abe Vigoda, at the Drew Carey Roast—1998

I'm very relaxed. I was completely—not confident that I was gonna do well, you never are because you could die in those rooms really easily—but I knew that I knew how to put this Roast together. I think that these guys just feel like some cute little girl can't possibly do it, which I think that I've proven differently at this point."

Jon Lovitz joked that day about how Aiello never ages: "We met twelve years ago. I was twenty-eight and he was fifty-five. Now I'm forty and he's fifty-seven. A few more years and I'll be old enough to be his father."

After surveying the room, Sandra Bernhard said, "I don't recognize the old Jewish Friars here today. Usually when I meet them in hotel rooms they're wearing terry cloth robes." Bernhard also shared, "I worked with Danny in *Hudson Hawk*. I

was straight when I worked with him and slept with him. He wore lace panties and a push-up bra. I didn't want another man after that."

"Danny is so strong, he was the only pallbearer at John Candy's funeral," joked Dick Capri.

While Jeffrey Ross was speaking, nature apparently called Aiello, because he left the dais. Ross joked that he was getting nervous, thinking the actor left to make plans to have him off-ed. He spoke to the empty chair, "It's a real honor for me to be here today. I'm a fan of your work—especially your recent project." Freddie Roman then donned a pair of Aiello-esque sunglasses and jumped into the empty hot seat so Ross could finish his act to a warm body.

"That was one of the greatest Roasts that the Friars, in my experience, have ever had," Joy Behar says. "Not just because I was hosting it, that's not the reason. The reason was Danny Aiello as the subject. There's a guy whose ego is bigger than his schlong. So what you've got is a perfect specimen, because you can make fun of his ego and his egotism. Then, at the same time, you could also do what Belzer did, which was read the worst review he ever got. So, you deflate him at the same time as you're getting laughs, because no one really feels sorry for him. It's a marvelous combination.

"I've known Danny for a while, and he's a lot of fun. He's a perfect target. I mean, when you do these Roasts, a lot of times I don't want to do them because I don't know the subject. I did Drew Carey, and I had a hard time because I didn't know Drew Carey. I didn't have a grip on it, so I'll never do that again. I learned. You have to know them and like them. It's important.

"For some reason, it's also not as much fun if you don't like the person. Because then you border on the mean and vicious. And when a Roast gets vicious and mean, nobody laughs. You have to also know that the subject is okay with everything you're saying for everybody to feel comfortable."

"I was apprehensive about today," announced Aiello when he accepted his Roast award. "It's an unusual feeling to sit and have people throw insults at you." Talk about understatements.

ROASTING STILLER

Of all of the people who have been roasted over the last century, none seems a more unlikely candidate than that humble cherub, Jerry Stiller. His Roast took place in 1999. "When I was asked to be roasted I told Kenny Greengrass, 'I don't belong up here, why me?' And he said, 'Because people love you. You're popular.' It was also, of course, because of *Seinfeld*, and I was playing the Frank Costanza character. I was kind of riding the crest with that show. Ken said, 'People will say funny things about you, you'll laugh. You'll be part of it.' Finally, he said, 'There's so many people who want to honor you, they love you.' Well, when you hear that word all of a sudden it's like everything is wiped away. It's like we're going to make you the president of

Jerry Stiller is serenaded by Jason Alexander at his Roast — 1999

Sandra Bernhard turns up the heat and Jerry Stiller dances (or something) at his Roast — 1999

the United States and you don't have to run for office. And my ego just let me be swept away into this wonderful night that they offered me."

Judging from his comments on the dais that night, Alan King was just as confounded by the choice of this guest of honor in 1999: "Why are we honoring this bore? A man who gave up a career as a male model. He wasn't really our first choice, but we found out too late that Abe Vigoda was alive. Not only are you fucking dull, you're fucking old." And this was at the beginning of the

Roast! Jerry had an entire evening ahead of him.

Jason Alexander was the roastmaster. He began the show by serenading Jerry with a funny song about getting a call from the Friars asking him to roast a "Jerry." His answering machine cut out before he could hear Jerry who, so he surmised every Jerry in the book—none of them Stiller, of course. "The Friars Club has a long and distinguished tradition of paying tribute to the very finest entertainers in our history," Alexander told the audience. "Tonight they've broken with that tradition and are honoring Jerry Stiller."

Stiller recalls: "About three or four days before the Roast I suddenly started to sweat and got very nervous. I thought, what am I gonna do? What am I gonna say? They were going to hit me with everything under the sun. How was I going to respond? It will be terrible. I don't know how to deal with it. But it was too late to back out."

And this Roast was not just for the Friars but also would be airing on Comedy Central. It was the second Roast the cable comedy channel taped for public viewing, having had great success with the Friars Roast of Drew Carey the year before.

Stiller rose to the occasion, however, and entered the ballroom that night, "It was an incredible moment when they marched me down with these beautiful, mostly naked women, and they sat me in this big red chair. It was blazing; it was like it was the devil's roost or something. Alan King got up and started to let go with his funny zingers, and all I remember is being so uncomfortable. I didn't know what to do, and I just was reacting naturally because that was the true me, and I guess people responded to just watching a guy squirm."

Thanks to this event Susie Essman is busy working on a hit HBO show. "It was actually the Friars Roast that got me the part on *Curb Your Enthusiasm*, the Stiller Roast. Because Larry David saw it on Comedy Central, called me up, and gave me the job. That's how I got the part. Larry had this scene in mind where Jeff, my husband on the show, brings this Fresh Air Fund kid into our house and he robs us blind. He said to me, 'I just want you to rip Jeff a new one.' I think that when he saw me on the Roast he was like, she can handle destroying somebody. That's what he had in mind. He wanted me to destroy Jeff, and he saw me destroy every old Jew on that dais."

The night of the Roast, as Essman explains, she was not feeling a hundred percent: "I had laryngitis. I couldn't speak, and I'm sitting there next to Danny Aiello. Luckily he was talking so much I didn't even have to respond. But literally no sound. It's every comic's nightmare. I've had that nightmare where I'm onstage and I open my mouth and no sound comes out. I had infectious laryngitis, and no sound was coming out of my mouth and it was quite anxiety-provoking. I said, 'I have to apologize, Jerry knows why, I know why, enough said.' It wasn't pretty."

Kevin James, who co-stars with Stiller on *King of Queens*, also spoke at the event. "When they asked me to do this Roast, I was really intimidated because this is not my forte," he told the audience. "I'm really not great at saying mean-spirited things about people I love, like Jerry Stiller. Fortunately the writers on my show don't feel the same way. . . . Can somebody please tell me how a guy can screw up the line 'Good morning, Douglas' ten times in a row, and yet one night a week the man stands in front of a group of total strangers and has no trouble with 'Hi, my name is Jerry and I'm an alcoholic'?. . . This one's actually from our co-star Leah Remini. She couldn't be with us tonight, but she sends her congratulations on your Roast and says to relax, have a great time, and P.S. don't worry, her special friend finally showed up."

Stiller survived. "I see the re-runs of it, and I watch Jason Alexander as a classic roastmaster," he says. "He had taken the time to write the most brilliant material, which made me feel like I really belonged. I almost wanted to cry it was so funny. Then came the moment where I said, 'Do I answer back?' I didn't have anything to say, and thank God Sandra Bernhard came on singing some wacky rock 'n' roll song. I didn't know what to do, and she kind of gyrated, and I started to gyrate with her. I started to move with her body and kind of try to emulate her, and that seemed to save my day. I don't consider myself a dancer, but I suddenly found bones in my body that reminded me of the Nicholas brothers. I just kept moving and it got some response.

"When it was over I was relieved, and yet at the same time I could not get over the response that I got from that audience and the fact that I had made it with the Friars somehow. I was considered somebody in the business. The appearances of Anne, Amy, and Ben on the dais got to me. Some of the legends were on the dais—performers, public figures, people who surely had a life but took the time. I was overwhelmed by their presence that night. I look back and thank everyone who gave of themselves. To give of your talent to another performer is a gift. That night will never leave me."

REVENGE ON BELZER

What goes around comes around, and in 2001 Richard Belzer got his comeuppance for making

Al Franken and Richard Dreyfuss take a breather from the dais of the Rob Reiner Roast—2000

other roastees cry. Just as he was about to march onto the dais he said, "I was scared, then I was relaxed, then I got scared again, now I'm feeling calmer because I'm sensing that in spite of what anyone says tonight, there's going to be a lot of love in the room."

He was so wrong. "Richard Belzer is the man who made you laugh so much and then stopped around 1991," joked roastmaster Paul Shaffer. The roastmaster's tirade continued throughout the evening. "I met him twenty-seven years ago," Shaffer said of Belzer. "That was when he still considered heroin one of the four basic food groups."

Alan King said, "He used to be funny, and he's been on a cop show for nine years. So what I thought I would do, for the sake of entertainment, is read my own biography." And he did!

Bill Maher told of how Belzer became his mentor and role model: "Little boys growing up have their heroes and little girls have their heroines—I have heroes on heroin."

Dom Irrera said, "I was fucking Belzer in the ass one day. Not in a gay way—like a Viking. I had my hands on the horns of his metal helmet."

"It's true, you roast the ones you love," says Susie Essman, talking about this Roast. "Roasting Belzer was a pleasure because he's one of my closest friends—and I was brutal with him. That was a really fun one for a lot of reasons. It was in a theater, which was a great venue, it was not televised, and everybody who roasted him was a close friend. It had that flavor of the old-time Roasts. We were all his close friends, so it's completely appropriate for me to talk about his wife being a soft-core porn star or however I wanted to destroy him personally. Because he's a good friend, I can do it."

Rapper Ice T, Belzer's co-star on *Law & Order SVU*, looked around the all-white dais and said,

Bill Maher gets Richard Belzer at Belzer's Roast—2001

"The last time I looked at a box like this I was on fucking trial for murder."

This Roast may not have run on Comedy Central, but it was in a theater with members of the general public in attendance. As Freddie Roman presented Belzer with his award, he said, "Richard, the Friars never open the doors of our Roasts to let the public see firsthand what goes on here. But we have so little respect for you that we wanted to share every painful moment with everyone in this theater tonight. It has been an honor watching you squirm."

"Thank you, I am really touched," said Belzer. "All I can say is I wish I had gotten bigger stars. I wish it had been Carnegie Hall instead of Town Hall."

A TRIBUTE TO HEF

In the fall of 2001 Hugh Hefner took his place on the roasting spit. He recalls: "It really is a celebration. It's insult comedy. The truth of the matter is they were tougher on one another than they were on me. There were some lines there for people who weren't necessarily expecting it. But it's the nature of insult comedy, and I think that what makes it really delightful is we live in a kind of politically correct society, and this is kind of like friends getting together and breaking the rules."

Roastmaster Jimmy Kimmel knows all about breaking rules: "What could you say about Hef that hasn't already been mumbled incoherently by

Hugh Hefner brought his girlfriends—and one for good measure—for support when the Friars roasted him in 2001

a thousand young women with his cock in their mouths?"

Hefner strolled into the Hilton ballroom with seven blondes arm in arm in arm in arm in arm in arm in arm. He recalls: "I took the girlfriends, and it was a nice trip to New York. It's a trip I don't make very often because it kind of requires a special occasion to do it. We just had a very good time."

The comedians had a good time as well with his entourage, as Kimmel joked, "I've read just about every issue of *Playboy* since I was fifteen years old and not once did I ever see a Playmate say one of her turn-ons was fucking a seventy-five-year-old man."

The theme continued with Jeffrey Ross: "I think it's awesome that you sleep with seven women, because eight would be ostentatious." Ross then explained why he needs to date that many women at one time: "One to put it in and the other six to move you around."

This Roast was held less than a month after 9/11 and almost didn't happen. "I think there was a recognition of the fact that the first thought was, well, we can't hold an event like this right after 9/11," explains Hefner. "And the second thought, which I think was the correct one, is that we must hold it because otherwise the enemies won. This is the way you honor the dead—by celebrating life, by not allowing terrorism to dramatically curtail or change the nature of your life. And certainly, what is more all-American than a Roast? I mean, it breaks the rules. It's free speech taken to the nth degree."

Freddie Roman announced at the beginning of the show, "For the Friars, this is normal—telling dirty jokes, making fun of people—it's what we do and we're proud to do it for you so that you can get some laughter back into your life and into your hearts." The Friars Club, the Friars Foundation, Comedy Central, and Hefner himself all contributed what amounted to $550,000 to the World Trade Center Fund through this event.

But comedy still reigned supreme.

"Hugh Hefner, who likes to be called Hef—but

Hugh Hefner with his roastmaster, Jimmy Kimmel—2001

*Cedrick the Entertainer, Dr. Joyce Brothers, and Vincent Pastore (*The Sopranos *"Big Pussy") make an interesting threesome at Hugh Hefner's Roast—2001*

in Hebrew, spelled backwards, it's Feh!" said Alan King.

"This night is dedicated to the man who made jacking off a national pastime," said Kimmel.

"He has fondled more playmates than Michael Jackson," said Ross.

Drew Carey asked the girls who were seated in front of the dais, if being with Hef was "like fucking a skeleton wrapped in wax paper. How do you even know when he cums? Does dust come out?"

Despite the humor, there was a pall hovering over the ballroom that evening. "I think, at first, people were afraid to make any references, and then a few came out. It helped lighten people up a little in a very ironic way," says Hefner. Rob Schneider said, "We're here tonight to honor a man who personifies why these terrorists hate us. If it were up to them, women wouldn't read, couldn't work, get fake tits, go to school, pose nude to help their career. Hugh Hefner believes women should be able to do all those things—except read."

At one point Jeffrey Ross bounded up to the podium after one of Schneider's jokes may not

have flown. Ross asked, "Hasn't there been enough bombing in this city?" Suddenly the topic that comedians had been avoiding for two weeks was now fair game, and the audience realized they were allowed to just sit back and enjoy the Friars doing what they do best—making people laugh via their unorthodox humor.

Gilbert Gottfried screamed, "Hugh Hefner does-

Paul Shaffer gets a lift in his musical number to Chevy Chase at Chevy's Roast—2002

n't need Viagra, he needs cement!" But he, too, dipped into the well of newfound topics: "Tonight, I'll be using my Muslim name, Hasn't Been Laid!"

It wasn't all about sex and dirty jokes, however. For Hefner a memory still lingers: "I think the most touching moment, in part because it was such a contrast, was that Dick Gregory played it from the heart rather than for humor. He was the first standup black comedian to appear in a non-black venue and that occurred in the early 1960s at the Playboy Club in Chicago. It broke the color line; there were singers and musicians who had performed before, but not standup comics. Redd Foxx, Richard Pryor, Slappy White, and all of those guys played a black circuit of clubs, but not white clubs. That changed with the Playboy Club and with Dick Gregory, and he talked about that. He said, which I thought was over the top but was still very touching, 'You're my Martin Luther King.' It was very moving for me."

When it was over and the dust of what was left of Hugh's deflated ego cleared, Freddie Roman said, "Well, Hugh, I think the comedians proved beyond a shadow of a doubt that you're pretty much the biggest schmuck in the room."

All this talk and Hefner still looks back fondly on the day: "I think it was the legacy of the Friars and the history of it that I was very much aware of. I felt honored to be invited to be a part of it because the Friars' members and those honored and roasted in the past have been my heroes—those people who influenced me when I was a kid. So it was very memorable for me."

BROTHERLY LOVE

It was only a matter of time for the Friars to catch up with the controversial Tom and Dick Smothers, and they finally did in 2003. "They said, they're really going to take you apart and don't take it personally," says Tom Smothers of the event. "I was told by someone who had been to many of them, 'Remember, you're expected to really get back at them. Don't be a good guy. Get back at them.' So I was prepared for that, and then everyone was so nice. I thought they'd be screaming at us."

The comics may not have been screaming, but Roastmistress Susie Essman is certainly capable of doing so. Originally the roastmaster was to have

Judy Gold roasting Tom and Dick Smothers at the Brothers' Roast—2003

been Richard Belzer, but a few days before the Roast his television-shooting schedule changed. The deal with the Friars is, if you have a paid gig, go do it. "That was a last-minute thing," says Essman. "If I had been asked originally I probably would have said no because I didn't know them. Even though they're part of my childhood in a way, I knew of them and I knew their body of work and I knew a lot of people on the dais. Luckily, I had some great writers working with me, helping me. I had like four or five days' notice to do that."

But she did it. "I was talking to somebody about your career the other day and all of a sudden out of nowhere a fat lady started singing." This line was one of the more sedate zingers she threw in the brothers' direction. "I think the reason why I pulled

it off and did so well is because I had so much experience doing it. It really makes a difference because I had done so many Roasts, and then the tributes. A tribute to this, that, and the other one. It's a skill that you develop, like anything else. So I think that came into play for the Smothers Brothers Roast, and I was able to just focus and do it because I had done so many before."

"You gotta be a little bit outta your fuckin' mind to sit here and let everybody throw shit at you for two hours," bellowed Alan King, who definitely had a point. Alan also came prepared with inside information. "In doing my research I found out that they're twins and that they were conjoined at birth—connected by their cock. Now, the surgeon, not being a Solomon, gave one a little more cock than the other. That's why he's going through life known as Tiny Tom and he's the big Dick."

Stewie Stone noted, "I thought old gentiles were handsome. You look like German U-Boat commanders. It's a delight to be on the dais honoring you guys, 'cause you are trailblazers, and you did have something to say years ago. And now the best you could hope for is Kutcher's, Labor Day."

Dom Irrera honed in on the Brothers' talents: "The Smothers Brothers, I gotta say, are the best comedy team of all time. Except for Abbott and Costello, Laurel and Hardy, Cheech and Chong, Mack and Zack, Mack and Jamie, two guys I saw at the Improv the other night, and Louie Anderson. How clever they were. This is unprecedented, by the way in comedy, they had one guy who played the smart guy, get this, and the other guy played it dumb. Now, nobody has ever done that before except for Abbott and Costello, Laurel and Hardy, Cheech and Chong, Mack and Zack, Mack and Jamie, Frick and Frack, Tom and Jerry, and Louie Anderson."

"That was so fun," says Judy Gold. "I'm sitting next to Chuck Scarborough, and my first joke was about him, so we were chit-chatting and I'm like, 'Okay, I just have to tell you my first joke is about you,' and he didn't even care. It was great. You have lunch with these people that you would never meet. You know what's so great about it? When you're at the Friars Club you're all the same. It's just this

Susie Essman gets roasted herself when Tom and Dick Smothers get even with the roastmistress—2003

common denominator, and you just feel like, wow I've arrived, I'm a member of this club."

Judy realizes that if you have a funny joke, don't toss it, "There was one joke, I said, 'I feel so uncomfortable that Abe Vigoda has been undressing me with his cataracts.' That was actually going to be for Joe Franklin who ended up not being on the dais but sat in the audience."

Tom Smothers didn't realize that before they throw you to the lions, the Friars give you a cocktail party backstage: "I thought that was the greatest part of it. I thought it was just a lunch. I didn't know it was going to be that big of a deal, and then the publicity backstage and meeting all these people who I've never met before. I liked it. It made a big impression on me. That this was not to be taken lightly, this was quite an honor. We both liked it. We were both very impressed."

Tom tried to make peace with the firing squad beforehand: "I went down the whole dais before it happened, during the lunch. I went down the whole thing and shook hands and said hello to every single person on the dais. It was great."

Maybe visiting with each dais member paid off after all, because the Brothers may have had to edit a few things in their speech afterward. As Tom recalls: "We had some hardcore jokes to throw at them, but I did one joke and then I backed out because it didn't seem appropriate. They were all so polite. You can't say, 'Hey, you cocksuckers,' after they were pretty nice. I really expected to be beat up worse. So what one always does at something like this, when you don't know what is going to happen, you play the moment. You can't choreograph a bullfight, and I kind of had it choreographed, but, I said, 'Well, I better get out of this one, play it a little softer.'"

It's a rare moment when things are considered soft for this group, but that's the beauty of being one hundred years old—you're allowed to just do what you damn well please. Their dinners and Roasts serve a valuable service—they make people laugh, cry, and just get lost in that feel-good place of showbiz called the Friars Club.

CHAPTER SEVEN

THE FRIARS ARE IN THE HOUSE

Behind Closed Doors at the Monastery

"Give me a table near a waiter!" was Henny Youngman's greeting when he would enter the main dining room of the Friars Club. This famous quote still echoes through the nooks and crannies of the building the Friars lovingly refer to as the monastery. That one-liner sums up life in the club and all that is good about these funny, demanding, and often hungry characters. They crave attention and camaraderie, not to mention a good corned beef on rye.

"You need a place to have a drink and see a couple of guys. We had such great characters here," says Alan King, who has been hanging out in various Friars locales for decades.

One never knows what to expect walking through those

Opposite page: Friars "Kibitzing" at the monastery, in a cartoon that appeared in a club publication—1930s

doors, as King soon discovered. "I remember the Edison. I was eighteen years old, and I came in and the first thing I saw, in one of those big gothic chairs, the great Willie Howard was sound asleep," he says. "This was lunch. Dead drunk and sound asleep. He was one of my early idols, and that's the first time I saw Willie. And the guys were terrible to him. He'd have a few boozes and he'd fall asleep. They warned him if he fell asleep he'd be sorry. So after ten warnings, a whole bunch of guys took chewing gum, everybody started chewing, and they put the gum on his nose, on his chin, and one piece of gum on his cheek. Then they stuck paper matches in each one, and they lit it, and they hollered FIRE! Then he woke up. The son of a bitch was four blocks away before he realized what was going on. Oh, they used to do terrible things to people."

Practical jokes seemed to be the norm around the monastery. Just ask Harry Delf, Jr. about a certain special event at the Friars. "Commodore Day was the day when a new member was appointed commodore of a picnic," he recalls. "The guy would spend a couple of months getting a whole thing going, and nobody would ever show up. That was their kind of sense of humor. It's funny, unless you spent a lot of time on it. They did things like that. They always played practical jokes on other people. I think that was something that went back all the way into the teens."

Delf tells his own story of being a victim of the Friars' wacky sense of humor: "They pulled a practical joke on me once. I used to go up and meet my father at the club at

Membership has its privileges and one of them is to keep in style with Friarly fashions. Left: Jerry Lewis had a great time at the photo shoot selling the Friars Club baseball jackets

Above: Susan Lucci is the prettiest of the Friars models, showing off a Friars Club jacket. Ed Sullivan obviously enjoys things from his perspective as well

Above right: Frank Sinatra and the Friars Club hat. For the record, the cigarette is not a Friars Club Cigarette, although they did have their own brand in 1907

Ken Greengrass, Freddie Roman, Drew Carey, and Alan King smile for the camera after lunching at the Friars Club — 1998

the Edison. They had a pool table and a card room all on this one floor. So I used to play pool waiting for my father to finish playing gin. This guy walked over and asked me if he could join me, and I was like thirteen or something and thought I was pretty good. Turns out to be Andrew Ponzi, who was considered to be the best pool and billiard player ever, and he's missing intentionally—and I'm trying to beat him. Finally he started one of his famous runs, and the whole club was in hysterics watching me. He was doing shots, jumping the balls, going all over the place, all kinds of things. They finally admitted it to me. But they used to set up people all the time—members, the old-time members, especially the new members—they would get them."

Friars Club Historian Bernie Kamber, a press agent who remembers the Edison and even earlier

times, says, "Comedians can be kind of cruel. I was a sucker for them." Kamber laughs when talking about how Groucho Marx and his cronies used to sit in the dining room telling jokes with no punch lines. While everyone around him laughed, Kamber was clueless. "I would laugh because I didn't want them to look at me funny, but I had no idea what the joke was," he says. It's a no-brainer in the Friars' timeline to see how their joking antics were eventually elevated to their most honored of events—the Roast.

VIRGIN VOYAGES

Coming to the Friars Club for the first time is an experience, to say the least. The building alone is worthy of an *Architectural Digest* article. (Of course, most magazines are funny about using four-letter words, so the Friars may not be on the top of their list.) But most people agree there is something to be said about their first trips to the monastery. Norm Crosby explains, "It's the intimacy, the closeness. It's people who are in the grocery business, people who are plumbers, butchers, and doctors—'Hey, Norm!' Even if they don't know you, 'Hey, Norm!'—and by the time you get to your table, you want to take your clothes off. You feel like you're in your house. I can't explain it. It's just a wonderful, nice feeling that you get when you come into the building. That's a tribute to the staff, Jean-Pierre Trebot, to the people that really make this club work, and the membership, of course. They must feel it when they walk in, so they impart it to other people. It's phenomenal—and it's really just something special."

Freddie Roman had to prove his mettle before he could strut around in his Friars blazer—not that he wasn't up to the task. "I absolutely remember my first time in the building," he says. "I had just been accepted to membership, and I walked up to the second-floor bar, and Alan King was holding court with Buddy Hackett. I knew Alan a little bit, Buddy not at all, and there was a whole group of guys standing there. And Alan said, 'Oh, this is a new Friar, comedian Freddie Roman.' And Buddy said, 'Oh, you're a comedian?' I said, 'Yes.' He said, 'Where do you work?' I said, 'Catskill Mountains.' He said, 'Oh, well, tell us a joke. We'll tell you if you're a comedian.' That's very intimidating—and there were a whole group of guys standing there. And I told a joke and he said, 'Okay, you may be a comedian someday.' It was funny, and everybody was laughing. But it was a little frightening. I had to audition for the right to be able to stand at the bar with them.

Joy Behar broadcast several of her popular radio shows from the Friars Club. This segment was with comedians Freddie Roman, Stewie Stone, and Bobby Shields—1991

"As the evening progressed, they asked me to join them for dinner, which really was a wonderful thing for me to be in their company. That started off my feelings of camaraderie about the club, and to this day, when a young comic comes in I immediately try to bring them into conversation. I don't ask them to tell a joke, though."

Susan Lucci's first time at the monastery was for lunch as the guest of a member. "I got to see that great group of comedians. I was lucky enough to be there one afternoon when they were all there—Milton Berle, Henny Youngman, Joey Adams—and I got to see that in action," she says. "Not that I sat at the same table, but next to them. It was thrilling because they were legends, and Freddie Roman and Pat Cooper were there and—just to hear them banter back and forth—it was a gift I didn't expect. It was a treasure to be able to sit there in their presence like that.

"It seemed very New York to me, in the best sense of the word. This New York brownstone—it's a building where you feel history. I feel that when I walk into Radio City Music Hall, and I certainly felt that when I walked into the Friars Club. Not only the history of the building, but the history also of another time, when the comedians like Henny Youngman and Milton Berle and Freddie Roman appeared in the Catskills, which was over by the time I came into the business. It was so wonderful to hear that borscht belt humor, and it was fabulous."

Joy Behar credits booking agent Ruth Stern with much of the club's success in extending invitations to new types of members. "Ruth Stern, I think, is the one who pretty much is responsible for getting some of the younger women in," Behar says. "She used to have these lunches. There was a kind of movement to get comedians in, to get women in, so I was at that point. I was quite taken with what it looked like. It really looks like a monastery. I think I was waiting for Friar Tuck to arrive—or some guy in a dress, at the very least."

What's refreshing about Friars is their blatant honesty, as Behar recalls all too well in talking about her first trip to the monastery: "There was Joey Adams drooling at one table and Gene Baylos drooling at another table. It reminded me of my house, of my Italian family at Thanksgiving, when they'd all fall asleep after the high-tryptophan dinner, and they'd all be drooling. They'd fall asleep in the chairs, and it was sort of like that. Who else was drooling? Oh, Professor Irwin Corey. I don't know how old he is now, but he doesn't seem to change. He's still sharp as a tack. So, it's people like him who were around, and I was kind of taken with that. I think that the maitre d', Frank Capitelli, who greets you at the door, is just the most warm, loving person. I mean, he's adorable."

LeRoy Neiman looks at the monastery differently than the comedians do, because he has the perspective of an artist. "Before I was a member, people would take me there once in a while, and I was always impressed, like most people are when they go there," Neiman says. One of his first visits to the monastery was for the Friars' traditional Friday lobster night. "I remember one night this young actress kind of girl who was with this man who was probably a producer, in my mind, sitting there and tying his bib on him. I made a sketch of it. I just made a drawing, and that to me for some strange reason has always been a symbol of the Friars Club. The actress and the producer—that's way-back kind of thinking, but it's still there.

"I'm a misfit every place I go, because I'm a fraternizing friendly artist, and that kind of stuff is my beat, you might say. That's what I like to draw and paint, and I express myself through experi-

The Friars' distinguished resident cartoonists and artist; Ranan Lurie, Al Hirschfeld, and LeRoy Neiman — 1995

ences there. I haven't seen any digression at all since my first impressions, and every time I go there people are friendly and they're always happy to be there. That's the main thing—they're not there to eat—they're there just to be and meet all these people. I used to sit there with Broadway producer Irv Welzer, and Henny and Belzer, and all those people. It was a great bunch. There were times when I didn't dare open my mouth because I felt I wasn't up to it, but then I realized over a long time that they're great people."

Richard Lewis first came to the Friars Club as a guest of Alan Zweibel, who at the time was a writer for *Saturday Night Live*. Lewis says he felt right at home: "When I first walked into the Friars Club, before I was a member, I felt I belonged there. When I was looking at all of the amazing photos on the walls as a young comedian, I hoped that maybe one day mine would be there, too, and people would say, 'I can't believe Richard Lewis is a member here.' Now, I can only hope that some young performer is thrilled to see my photo up

there and dream of one day being a member like I once did. Still, after all I've done in show business, it's very hard even now to look at a picture of Frank Sinatra and Orson Welles and not feel like, 'What table should I bus?'"

Those photos have an impact on many people when they see them for the first time, agrees Susie Essman: "It was Joy Behar who dragged me. She said, 'You have to come to the Friars Club.' It was some radio thing we were doing, and it was like Mickey Freeman and Mal Z. Lawrence, and I don't remember who else, and it was upstairs. That was the first time I was ever there. The thing I remember as being the most impressive, besides the fact that it's such a beautiful space, were the photographs on the walls. I remember just being mesmerized by the history of show biz in those photographs. I mean, where else do you see photographs of Sophie Tucker and Al Jolson and Dean Martin and Frank Sinatra all together? I remember being quite struck, and those gorgeous black-and-white prints. I was just fascinated by the photographs."

Judy Gold concurs: "To this day, when I walk in there, I still look at those pictures on the wall, and it's like I'm looking at them for the first time. I love it. When I look at that I think, 'Wow, look at the talent that this place has had.' And now my picture is up!" Okay, so it's near the bathroom in the basement, but that's not the issue, and Judy knows it. An honor is still an honor.

Even Joan Rivers takes her monastery experience seriously. "I think it's a wonderful place," she says. "When you look at the history and you look at the pictures on the walls, it's such a celebration of funny people, and funny people are so third-rank. You know that? My mother would never say I was a comedian; she would always say, 'She's a writer.' I mean, we're the ones who make the world happy."

NO PLACE LIKE HOME

Jeffrey Ross has a theory as to why the monastery is such a coveted place to so many people. "Comedians get lonely," he says. "When you work the road as much as I do it's nice to know there is a place to come home to where people are happy to see you. The dining room is like *Cheers*—everybody knows your name. When I first became a member, Henny Youngman would come in every day and eat lunch at the same table. Frank, the maitre d', would always greet him like the superstar he once was. Young members would kneel beside his wheelchair and pay their respects. It made me proud to be a comedian."

That dining room has seen a lot, and Jan Murray tells of having a ringside seat to some of the madness: "You know, with Gene Baylos, off stage he was the funniest man there was. On stage he didn't have the nerve to do what he did off stage. I hadn't been in New York for about four or five years, and I came in to do something. Of course, whenever I came to New York after I moved out to California, I always came to the Friars for dinner or to have lunch with people. I'm sitting there with my wife this one night—we were having dinner before going out to see a show. I ordered chicken, there's bread, there's all kinds of food in front of me, and Baylos walked in.

"I hadn't seen him in years. I said, 'Gene, how are you?' He never said hello—he started right in. He said, 'I just came back from California. I did *The Tonight Show*. I had to come back here to go to the Concord. Then I must run right back to California to do *The Dean Martin Show*. MGM wants me for a picture.' Well, if you know Gene, you can't imagine him doing one of these shows. He used to work in these broken-down joints, so him saying all of this was hysterical! That was the text. The action that he did with it is what made it really down-on-the-floor laughing, because as he's saying it, 'Oh, just came back from the coast, did *The Tonight Show...*,' he picked up the roll and put it in his pocket. Each one that he said, he picked up whatever food was on my plate and put it in his pockets. He cleaned off my whole plate while he's telling me all these great jobs he had. That's hysterical. If you saw me do this physically, you would die laughing."

Jerry Stiller has spent a lot of fun days and nights at the monastery, and he still tells the story of one of his first visits to the club: "Soon after I was initiated I was sitting at a table with Henny Youngman and Gene Baylos at their behest. They were trying to entertain me, each trying to be funnier than

Gene Baylos clowns around with NYC Mayor Abraham Beame — 1980s

the other. They were doing shtick, and one would say, 'That was my piece. You took that from me.' Then Henny would pick up the plate with a saucer on it and try to drink the coffee with the plate and the saucer, and his hands were shaking and Gene said, 'That's mine! That's mine! You took that from me. I did that!' And Henny said, 'No, no, no, I'm the one.' Then we got out on the street and Gene walked up to a fire hydrant and started to mess around with it with his hands. He started to unscrew the hydrant, and he said, 'This is my vault.' Of course, the Chiclets came out of his mouth at one point too, and I thought, 'Gee, I'm

Friar Bill Clinton fits right in at the Friars Club — 2001

getting a private show here.' I think that I was being told, 'You can become one of us.' It was like a private show they were doing for me."

Gene Baylos performed at many Roasts and in-house events and became a Friars staple. One of his funniest routines was telling the story of a recent visit to the dentist, who did a great job, but as he was praising the dentist, his teeth would begin falling out, one by one. The cascading teeth were actually Chiclets, but the skit evolved into a hilarious bit that would have even Sinatra and Berle falling at his feet, crying with laughter.

Jean-Pierre Trebot tells another story about the infamous Gene Baylos: "Gene was a very good friend of Dean Martin's and even lent him money at a point when Dean was down on his luck. Dean never forgot that and had Gene appear on his television show on several occasions." Friars helping Friars—that's what the club is all about.

Judy Gold says one of her favorite memories from the monastery involves another classic Friar: "The thing I'll always remember is Henny Youngman sitting in that corner table, and one day I'm having lunch, and he's sitting there by himself. They give him a cup of coffee, and he picks it up and has his pinky out and takes a sip, and he puts it down. Then he picks it up again and on his pinky is, like, a spoon, and then he puts it down. Then he has a peppershaker on his pinky—and they just kept getting bigger and bigger, and no facial expression, nothing. It was so hilarious. 'Til he had, like, a bag hanging on his finger and he's delicately taking a sip of his coffee. I was cracking up."

While most Friars won't admit it, many of them have always gotten a kick out of having their names called over the P.A. system, connoting their Friarly status. Well, actually, a few of them *will* admit it. "When I joined I was so excited that I called about

Richard Lewis fretting on his very own chair, which is labeled "Prince of Pain" — 1998

ten people, and I had them page me in the dining room," says Richard Lewis. "They'd say, 'Friar Richard Lewis, Friar Richard Lewis, pick up the phone.' Now after the tenth call, Norman Fell, rest his soul, came over to my table. He knew me and was a fan of my comedy, as young as I was, and he—in no uncertain terms, in almost the same style as he kicked Dustin Hoffman out of the rooming house in *The Graduate*—says, and I'm paraphrasing, 'I want you out of this organization.' It was the exact same intonation. Then he hugged me, and he congratulated me on being a member. I will always remember that. He treated me like I

belonged there—and that was my first lunch."

Judy Gold has a similar story about being paged: "The greatest thing was after I became a Friar and they called me Friar Gold. I was like, 'Oh my God! I'm a Friar!' And then the best was, we used to call our friends to tell them to call us there so that I could get phone calls at lunch. That was the greatest: 'Friar Gold, line one.'"

Gold quickly learned a few other rules about the monastery, chief among them: Don't bring your mother to the dining room. "One time I brought my mother and my sister, and I said, 'Ma, don't stare at anyone,'" Gold recalls. "So we're sitting at the table—we were kind of in the back but not quite, like maybe the second or third table from the back wall—and I go, 'Oh, there's Alan King.' And she does this like entire-body move—meanwhile, she's always complaining she can't move—and she does an entire shift of the body and eyes. And I'm like, great, this is so embarrassing."

Richard Lewis also did the mother-at-the-Friars thing, which he says had its ups and downs: "My mom loved show business. My dad died young. She lived in New Jersey, and she had a boyfriend, and he loved the Friars, too. And when I was in town he would drive her into New York, and we would go to the Saturday brunch. My mother was very outgoing. I said, 'Mom, you gotta do me a favor. You cannot just walk over there. Let Henny finish his soup.' I was less afraid of Henny, but when Howard Cosell was alive I said, 'Mom, do me a favor, I beg of you. I have to go to the bathroom. Don't go over to Howard's table.' I loved Howard, but I said, 'He's a loose cannon.' I go to the bathroom. Where is she?

She's sitting right next to Howard, and Howard is doing a tirade on my mother to the entire room, but in his funny way. My mother was so star-struck that no matter who she saw, she mystically knew everything about their career and just ran over and praised them while I hid under the table.

"We would go up into the rooms on the second and third floor. And my dad was a very famous kosher caterer in North Jersey and in New York, and he was very close to a lot of the Friars and did a lot of their sons' bar mitzvahs—like Buddy Hackett's son and Joey Bishop's son. Bill Lewis was his name; he was the king of the caterers. Unfortunately, my dad died before I became a comedian. Otherwise, he would have been in heaven at the Friars Club because he knew so many of the people in those pictures and catered so many affairs for the people who were Friars. In fact, before Buddy Hackett died, we sat and talked at length about my father, and it was one of the nicest conversations I've ever had. It was a rush of memories."

Liz Winstead, Susie Essman, Judy Gold, and Joy Behar lunching at the monastery—2000

FOOD GLORIOUS FOOD

The Friars love to eat, making the main dining room the epicenter of the monastery. Let's face it: They named their biggest event after a side of beef, for heaven's sake. The Friars' fine dining has been making headlines for years, and even design flaws in the 48th Street monastery were deemed newsworthy, as evidenced in a 1927 issue of *Variety*, which noted: "The Friars' house committee has decided to move the dining room (known as the grill) from the rear of the first floor up to the main hall of the monastery. The grill has been found too warm in summertime. Its present space will be turned into a lounge and a reading room with light foods served after dining hours." A second mention of the same problem came in a 1933 *Variety* article about the Friars losing the 48th Street building. "The engine room is directly under the grill, with the result that in warm weather the spot was one of the city's hottest dining rooms," it reported. The flaw was sort of moot at that point, but such trivial mentions do prove that, throughout the club's history, at the monastery it's always been all about the food.

Frank Capitelli says he remembers Tom Jones dining at the club frequently. "He used to eat the beef stew and lamb stew," he reports. (Call the tabloids!) Frank also says that Spiro Agnew was a regular in the dining room, but he wouldn't share Agnew's favorite menu selections.

Buddy Clarke says the monastery was a home away from home for him. "I had dinner there every Friday night. I think it was $5.95 for two lobsters, all the clams you could eat, clam chowder, apple pie à la mode, and a beverage," he says. We all know the days of such low prices are long gone.

When asked about the Friars' food, Judy Gold can't give a straight answer: "I enjoy the Len

Top: *Alan Zweibel, Bill Murray, and Tommy Schlamme enjoy lunch in the Frank Sinatra Dining Room—1990s*

Bottom: *John Goodman chows down for lunch at the monastery with funnyman and former* Sgt. Bilko *cast member Mickey Freeman (he played Pvt. Zimmerman)—2000*

Cariou salad, chopped up with the vinaigrette—I enjoy the vinaigrette. I have no idea why there's fucking matzoh on the table in November. Why *is* there matzoh in the breadbasket in November? That's what I want to know."

Cy Coleman loves the food at the monastery, and he's not alone. "I bring Wendy Wasserstein to the Friars for lunch all the time," he says. "Whenever we make plans she always asks, 'We're eating at the Friars, right?' She loves the food

Lewis Black, Paul Shaffer, Dick Capri, Jerry Stiller, Ken Greengrass, and Danny Aiello enjoy a comedians' roundtable lunch at the Friars—1999

there. I always order the shrimp salad and now Wendy orders that too. She loves it."

Richard Lewis lives in Los Angeles, but he vows that when he returns to Manhattan full time, "I will know every pickle by heart there, by name!" Before he became sober, Lewis was on a liquid diet, but he behaved at the Friars Club. "One thing I'm proud of, I never made a fool of myself at the Friars," he says. "The Friars Club symbolized so much to me that I just did not want to look like an idiot there. Even in my heavy drinking days, I can almost swear that I never got drunk at the Friars Club for that reason. I just wanted to have some dignity and respect there. But once I wrote my book, *The Other Great Depression*, and people knew I was a recovering alcoholic, I would say to the former legendary bartender, 'Joe, give me seven Diet Cokes and line them up like soldiers.' So I probably looked more like an idiot sober than I did when I drank. I crazily did this to prove to people that I no longer drank. I had like a cavalry of diet sodas so everyone knows, 'Oh, there's Lewis. He has the entire Coca-Cola Bottling Company in front of him, but he's turned his life around.'"

Lewis says that he enjoys the food at the club, too. "In fact, when I'm under the weather I take a cab immediately and get the consommé, and then my seven Diet Cokes, of course," he says. "I've said to people, 'If I had to find one negative thing about eating at the Friars, it's that a lot of the people who go there every day tell the same stories.' So I had to change my technique in eating. Basically, it was eat on the run. But still I found that if I moved to different places in the Friars Club for an entire day, that these people would also follow me from room to room and begin the same show-business tale. In the course of eighteen hours I would only hear three stories, and it drove me crazy. It got unbearable to make-believe that I never heard this anecdote for the one-millionth time. To come clean, I do the same thing. I only have five stories. I've passed the big test for being a true Friar—I'm hilarious *and* repetitive. Now, granted—and I say this with deep affection—a lot of these stories were told by some of the elder statesmen, to put it mildly."

Perhaps Lewis's mother should have been made an honorary Friar, since the stories he has about her prove she fits right in. He says of taking his mother to brunch at the club: "My mother said it was the greatest spread she had ever seen in her entire life. One big problem with my mother is that she wouldn't let herself enjoy things. On her way in to the brunch on Saturday she would stop at some crappy diner before the Lincoln tunnel and eat. So she'd get to the Friars and say, 'I'm so full,' and then start picking from my plate, which of course would start a huge argument because she knew it disgusted me. That said, the brunch at the Friars is one of the great gifts from God. Even if my mother, rest her soul, only picked at it."

Sally Jessy Raphael found out the hard way that no one messes with the Friars' mess. In her capacity as prior of the Friars, she chaired a meeting that discussed the finances for their weekly brunch. Apparently, at that time they were spending more than they were making. "I decided that when I read this everybody would vote immediately to do away with Saturday brunch. Who wants to lose money selling bagels, lox, and cream cheese?" Raphael says. "I said, 'It's a big loss. We can't tolerate this kind of loss. We don't need this kind of loss. Besides, who eats brunch on Saturday, anyhow?' I suggested we do away with it. Well, by the time I came to, I was down on the street. So I asked the doorman, 'What did I do wrong?' He said, 'You tried to take food out of the mouths of Jews and Italians.' That's when I knew I was the only Puerto Rican member of the board. They called that meeting over faster than you've ever seen."

CARDS AND CHARACTERS

Of the varied areas throughout the club, one room stands out, a colony unto itself: the card room. Freddie Roman describes the room's significance: "A male bastion, no question about it—the card room and a bunch of characters here. There are guys here who have been playing cards for thirty-some-odd years. For good or bad, for a lot of them this is the reason they're here, because of the card room. A lot of interesting members of the club are card players. It's the same faces every day, and I equate it to—if a guy dropped dead in this card room, the game would continue and they'd just call EMS. It did happen, at the gin table. One of the Friars said, 'GIN!' and the guy fell back and he died. The game was pretty much over at that point. The card room is an integral part of the club.

THE GEORGE AWARD

Only a special few have been presented with the Friars' George Award—named in memory of George Burns and given to those carrying on his legacy of laughter. George himself was presented with the first George Award followed by Carol Burnett, Sid Caesar, Whoopi Goldberg, Bob Newhart, and Buddy Hackett.

Freddie Roman, Whoopi Goldberg, NYC Mayor Rudolph Giuliani, John Schreiber, and Alan King with Whoopi's Friars Club George Award—1997

Freddie Roman and Alan King present Bob Newhart with his Friars Club George Award—1998

"The first ten years I was never in there. Every member is within his rights to come here, but they don't until they get comfortable. You gotta get comfortable. A couple of new members who have come in the last couple of years just started coming in here now because it took them a little time to get used to the club. But then they're here. Gin rummy players are unique. There's nobody under fifty who plays gin rummy. It's a game that men have been playing for thirty, forty years, but no young people are playing it. Poker was younger. Our poker games, which have pretty much petered out, were a constant on Saturdays for thirty, forty years. But gin is the big card game at the club. Couple of pinochle players who have been here for a hundred years still play. Len Cariou plays gin."

Alan King says he used to play cards at the club, too. "I was a pretty good gin player," he recalls. "I used to play Lou Walters—he had one eye. But everybody used to pitch the 'out' cards to his bad eye, so he won maybe one out of four or five," King says. "I was a kid, and they used to set me up. Ted Lewis was a terrible gin player with a big temper. So I used to sit down and play him, and I'd be kibitzing, and I'd do everything to annoy him. He'd get pissed off. Finally, one time, I pick up, he throws, he discards it. I pick up a card, I throw it in, and I get up. He says, 'Where are you going?' I say, 'I'm going to the john.' He says, 'You gotta go to the john in the middle of the game?' I said, 'I've got to take a leak.' I put my cards face-down and I walk out. Outside, I pick up the phone, and I say, 'Page Ted Lewis.' There's a pause, and then 'Paging Ted Lewis' comes over the intercom. 'Hello?' he says into the phone. I say, 'Ted?' He says, 'Yeah.' I say, 'Gin!' And I hung up. He went crazy."

Jean-Pierre Trebot was well versed in the card players' compulsive tendencies from his predeces-

Socialite Aline Franzen, Susan Lucci, and Helmut Huber play cards at the monastery. Doubtful the game ended in fisticuffs like when the guys in the card room play— 1994

sor, Walter Goldstein. "Walter told me that when he was the assistant manager at the 56th Street monastery, that the card room was the largest department of the club," Trebot says. "He said that he would come in at nine in the morning and the card players would be just leaving the clubhouse! It never ceased to amaze him."

Frank Capitelli remembers the card room of the days when he first started at the club more than forty years ago. "There were two waiters working—one during the day, one in the night. The poker game, any kind of game, could go on 'til five o'clock, six o'clock in the mornings," he says. Who played? "Ted Lewis, Lou Walters—Phil Silvers was a heavy gambler. In those days he used to gamble

every single day. He had a Broadway show, and before the show he would be here gambling, then he used to go to the show. If he lost, you knew what kind of mood he was in—a very moody guy."

Capitelli says he discovered the obsessed mentality of the card players very early on. "One time we had a fire in the kitchen. The fire had been going on from Friday; now it's Saturday. We smell something burning, and we could not find out where it was coming from," he says. "We go around the building. All of a sudden, in the second-floor kitchen I open up the doors, and the room is full of smoke. So we call the firemen right away, we lock the elevator like they told us, we go upstairs, and I come up to the third-floor card room. I said, 'Gentlemen, we have to leave. We have a fire.' They couldn't see. Pitch black with smoke. They were still dealing cards. The firemen had to come up and throw them out.

"They don't budge," Capitelli continues. "They let this guy play—he had a wooden leg. So they called me to bring up oxygen because the guy passed out. You know the guy died? So we laid him out on the table and the wooden leg falls off. You think the other people stopped playing? They never stop for nothing, these guys. They're in a world of their own."

Some younger Friars do venture into the card room. Jeffrey Ross is one of them. "At first I was intimidated to be at the club," he says. "I was a guest invited to play poker. I didn't feel like I fit in. But eventually I realized that not only did I belong at the Friars, but hanging out with old Jewish comics was my destiny."

Stewie Stone is another regular in the card room. "It is the funniest thing in the world," Stone says. "In the Friars' card room are all these old rich, rich men that have nothing to do but play cards—and they fight over a penny. I'll say to them, 'With all your money, how can you fight over this?' And they'll say, 'But this is cash!' They scream and they holler, and

Nipsey Russell gets a bravo kiss from Sheila MacRae during the Friars salute to Gordon and Sheila MacRae — 1962

Steve Lawrence and Eydie Gorme open their Friars Club presents from Johnny Carson and Joe E. Lewis at their in-house salute — 1960

Joe E. Lewis bust dedication with sculptor Robert Berks, Ed Sullivan, Judge Abraham Lincoln Marovitz, and Buddy Howe — 1973

some of the guys say, 'Why can't we ever have a quiet game?' And my answer is, 'You want a quiet game, play with gentiles.' Jews love to scream. That's a Jewish thing—to scream."

In the summer of 2003, the entire northeast region of the country was hit with a major power failure. Afterward, the buzz question became: Where were you when the lights went out? Stewie Stone's answer to this question may be more entertaining than most. "During the blackout I was stuck in the elevator, and the card players continued to play by candlelight," he laughs. "I was stuck in the elevator with another gentleman, and the thing that made me the happiest was he was a Democrat. And I felt very good about that because if I was stuck in an elevator with a Republican, I would have been screaming and hollering. I didn't know it was a blackout in the whole city, so I thought they would get us out momentarily. I was thinking of all of these things we could do. I said, 'Let's get naked so when they open the elevator we'll come out naked.' That was the first fifteen

minutes. Then I started to get a little nervous. It started to get hot in there. And this is a new elevator! I'm saying, '$500,000 for an elevator and no key to open it?' The other elevator was worth $1.60, but we got everybody out.

"Finally, they opened the top and they said, 'Well, you can climb out the top, but what happens if the electricity goes on?' I said, 'It's been an hour and a half. What's the over and under on the electricity going on?' So when I climbed out the top, I look out and I see all these guys with their shirts off and candles lit. And they're playing gin rummy, while I'm stuck in the elevator. I wanted to kill them.

"There's the old joke about the avid golfers: They're playing golf and somebody asked one of

Eubie Blake's 99th birthday with some friends: Todd Cullen, Steve Karmen, William B. Williams, Sammy Cahn, and Blake — 1982

the guys, 'How was your golf game?' He says, 'What a terrible game playing golf with Harry. The sixth hole, he gets a heart attack and drops dead. What a terrible day—hit the ball, drag Harry, hit the ball, drag Harry.' So that was my gin game—hit the ball, drag Harry."

ACTIVE LOAFING

While the pool players do their thing just one floor down from the card players, Freddie Roman says the pool-playing Friars are a different breed from the rest. "That's become quite an interesting adjunct to the club," he explains. "The tournaments

are well attended and draw a tremendous amount of participation. They practice for hours. Fascinating."

There was a time when pool for the Friars was just as much an obsession as playing cards. Friar Bernie Kamber remembers times from monasteries gone by. "On 48th Street we had about ten pool tables and billiard tables," he says. "Bing Crosby was at the club all the time, and he had two hobbies there. One was playing handball on the three-wall handball court. That's a strange thing, but that's what we had on the top floor. But he also liked to shoot pool. That and card playing were big things in those days." Milton Berle also used to play pool, and Jerry Orbach and Paul Sorvino can sometimes be seen giving it their best shot during modern-day pool tournaments.

You're never too young to enjoy the Friars' pool experience, as Judy Gold can attest. "You know what was great? I brought Henry there, my seven-year-old, because I was doing one of those little comedy shows in the Milton Berle Room," she says. "We were supposed to go to a basketball game after, and we ended up going upstairs and having dinner with the other comics. Then Henry walked into the poolroom, and some of the Friars were in there playing—and they taught him how to play pool. He had the best time. He came home with the cigar smoke, smelling like shit. He went to school the next day, and the teachers called the department of child welfare. But it was great."

Speaking of cigars, what would the Friars be without them? If you thought they had problems with women coming into the club, imagine a city and state ban forcing cigars out of it! Thankfully, Milton Berle and George Burns aren't around,

Paul Sorvino taking his best shot in a Friars Club Pool Tournament at the monastery—1995

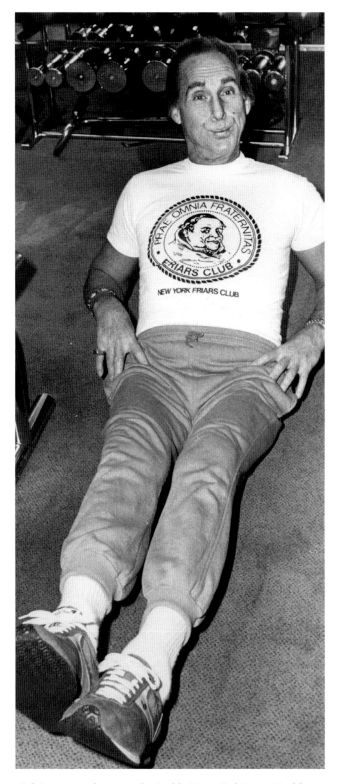

Sid Caesar works out in the Buddy Howe/Sal Greco Health Club — 1990s

though it's a pretty good guess that nothing would stop them from puffing away. "Cigar nights" were very special at the monastery, where Friars shared "a smoke and a joke." Interestingly enough, the jokes were far filthier than those told at any Roast. It may have taken a month for the smoke to clear, but around the monastery a good dirty joke lingers far longer than the aroma of a good cigar. Years later, laughs are still echoing off the walls from some of those nights.

The cigar nights still happen, though. Friars are not about to let a little law stop them from a well-honed tradition. They just moved the venue to a location where smoking is still allowed.

When smoking was in vogue, though, the Friars were chomping away daily. Buddy Arnold tells one of his favorite cigar stories: "Sid Gary, an old vaudevillian, he used to chew cigars, and Bing Crosby used to come into the club whenever he was in New York. This was the clubhouse on 56th Street. Bing used to smoke cigars at that time, and he'd chew them to a pulp. Then he'd walk up to you, if he knew you, and he'd take the cigar out of his mouth and shove it towards your lips and say, 'Have a puff,' and people would cringe and run away. Everybody would laugh. When he did it to Sid Gary once, Gary, in delight, took the cigar and put it in his own mouth and started to puff away. Disgusting sight, but what a scream he got. Crosby took it back, and he laughed with the rest."

The gym is a mainstay of the Friars and has been a staple of most of the various clubhouses. It may not be as popular as the card room—and, admittedly, the Barcaloungers probably get more of a workout than the biceps do—but there is no denying that today the Buddy Howe/Sal Greco Health Club is up to speed, as it features state-of-the-art equipment.

Stewie Stone, Jerry Stiller, Dominic Chianese, Freddie Roman, and Jack Carter help Freddie celebrate his tenth anniversary as Dean of the Friars — 2003

"In the gym we used to have beds," says Frank Capitelli. That alone speaks volumes about the Friars' exercise practices—at least when they first moved into their current building. "On one side of the gym there was a little room with about five cots where people used to relax and take a nap. These people would come over here, and they used to spend all day inside, so they'd go upstairs and take a nap. That's it. They still do that in the recliners, or watch TV or change, but in those days nobody used the gym. It became popular in the '80s."

Today, that medicine ball is getting much more use. Jeffrey Ross says he is not sure if you can include him as using the "gym" per se, but he has been in the area. "The good news is I once had sex in the steam room," he says. "The bad news is that I think it was with Freddie Roman."

John Ritter, Jan Maxwell, and Henry Winkler celebrate their Broadway show, The Dinner Party *with a Friars Club theater party — 2001*

CHAPTER EIGHT

OVER AND OUT—THE FRIARS' FIRST CENTURY

In-House Events and Monastery Madness

Opposite page: *Frank Capitelli, Alan King, Billy Crystal (taking a Roast-like stance), and Paul Shaffer at the ribbon (or something) cutting ceremony for the Friars' new Billy Crystal Bar—2003*

Friars say the darnedest things, and one never knows just what to expect upon entering the monastery. Susan Lucci gives one example: "I remember walking in, and I had on a knitted body suit, and Pat Cooper stopped me. He said to me, 'Susan, I have socks bigger than that body suit,' which made me laugh."

Richard Lewis also found his zinging moment at the monastery memorable. "The great Henny Youngman did something very funny to me, albeit unintentionally," he says. "I brought a very big financial manager to the club—he had never been there—and he went, 'Oh my God, there's Henny Youngman!' I said, 'Yeah, he's here every day.' He says, 'I gotta meet him.' So we walk over—and I had just done Letterman the night before and I killed. I mean, it was one

of the strongest shots I'd ever done on television. Now, to be truthful, my style of comedy is so antithetical to Henny Youngman's it's not even funny. I mean, I love one-liners and I write them, but nevertheless I'm far closer to Lenny Bruce than Henny Youngman. So here I am walking a childhood friend to Henny's table. I say, 'Henny, this is my friend Bob.' And he looks at me and says, 'I saw you last night. You don't do humor, do you?' I just lost it. My friend and I screamed because we knew exactly what he meant. He had no idea what I was talking about on television. Henny really came around to get it, though, because there were days when I would walk in after shots where he would give me a hug and say, 'You were very funny last night.' But early on it was a learning process."

INTIMATE AFFAIRS

Friars can always count on something going on at the monastery. Salutes, book signings, comedy nights, jazz nights, cabaret nights, cigar nights, holiday celebrations—anything for a party. The Friars traditionally welcome any opportunity to prove how much they love to honor each other. "I've done a bunch of tributes in the dining room," says Susie Essman. "I hosted Joy Behar's. They call them tributes, which is different from a Roast, but I kind of work them the same way. I'm not gonna do some schmaltzy tribute—I'm a comedian. I think that a lot of comedians take the tribute to mean they can do whatever material they feel like doing. It doesn't have to be about the person. The one we did two years ago for David Cone was fun because I'm such a baseball fan, so it's fun to write all that baseball material.

"We did the Freddie Roman one at the Danny Kaye Theater. That was fun. Joy Behar was the host. Roasting Freddie is just a blast. He's a cari-

cature of himself. He's one of the most roastable people I can think of. It's his enunciation—that rabbinical enunciation that he has and the kind of British lilt that he gets. He'll say At-lAntic Cit-ee, like we don't know he's a Jew from New York. Like all of a sudden we think he's from Connecticut or something."

Joy Behar has fond memories of the salute in her honor. "That was in the dining room, and all my friends got up and spoke lovingly about me and sweetly—I think," she says. "A few little jokes, a little ribbing—I think. Dom Irrera, who in my opinion is one of the funniest people working, was hysterical—you know why? Because he goes for it. Child abuse, sexual abuse, he's there, and he had us really rolling that day. He's one of my friends, and Susie Essman was there, and Kevin Meaney, Judy Gold, and Mario Cantone. They would say something about me, some crazy thing we shared together or whatever, and then they would go right into their act. They were hilarious, and that was lovely."

Behar also remembers being the mistress of ceremonies when the Friars honored Neil Sedaka. "I remember Kathie Lee Gifford was wearing some kind of animal print, and I told her *The Lion King* called and they wanted their costume back, or something like that," she says. "She was fine about it. But those kinds of things, those tributes, are semi-Roasts. Because comedians can't control themselves when they're in a tribute to anybody. It's like you've got to go for it." At that event, Behar went for it this way: "The reason we're so loose here tonight is because of you, Neil. Because you're so adorable. It's about you. . . . Did I sleep with you, ever? I never did, right? Even in the old days in Brooklyn?" Neil seemed to keep mum on that topic in response, but hey—the

Chicago *Producer and Oscar winner Marty Richards toasts Neil Sedaka at his Friars Club salute—2003*

Friars can be very incestuous, so you never know.

Another of Behar's memorable comments from that evening had nothing to do with Neil Sedaka—but that should come as no surprise to anyone who recognizes the musings of Friars. This is a sampling, however, of the Behar that Sedaka and company experienced that night: "I thought the Hasidim came over with Moses, but it's not true. Apparently, only two hundred and fifty years ago, some guy woke up in the middle of the Ukraine and he said to himself, 'Let's see, how can I serve my Lord *and* make a fashion statement? I know! I'll wear a big, big furry hat in the middle of August with a hot, hot woolen suit on a hundred-and-ten-degree day. It will have soup stains on it—it'll be fabulous.' And didn't it catch on? Look at the Amish. They picked right up on it. But they don't have the *payes*, 'cause you don't want them to get caught in the reaping machines."

Sedaka had a wonderful time, listening to the likes of Kathie Lee Gifford, Leslie Gore, Jane Olivor, and Billy Stritch sing the songs he wrote and made famous. He said that night, "The songs are like my children. They live and breathe, and tonight they all lived and breathed so beautifully." See? Sometimes the Friars can be serious, too.

Sedaka says of that evening, "It was a pleasure being honored by the Friars Club. I so appreciated all those that contributed to the success of the evening. Being a Friar is part of being in show business. I am very happy to be part of this renowned and respected club."

Composer Cy Coleman is a rare breed who has been wined and dined on multiple occasions by the Friars. He is a recipient of the Friars Foundation's Applause Award for Creative Achievement and was also the guest of honor at an in-house salute. "It was a very 'hamish' affair," says Coleman of his salute. For those Yiddishly challenged, he interprets: "That means it was such a good and warm night—such an honor. I really felt so welcome there." Coleman adds, "Even if it was a Roast, they insult the ones they love, so I wouldn't have minded that either."

Lucie Arnaz was there for both of Cy's tributes, and she served as the emcee for his in-house salute. "That meant a lot to me, because he's such a sweetheart," she says. "I appeared in his show *Seesaw*, and he wrote *Wildcat* with Carolyn Leigh for my mother, and we have a history together. We've been friends for a really long time, so I was honored to do that. The Friars Club is a wonderful organization; I love being asked to be a part of those events. They honor very worthy people, and their money goes to worthy causes."

Lest one thinks the Friars don't know from art and culture, LeRoy Neiman can prove otherwise. He says of being honored with a tribute in the monastery: "It's an honor. I've gotten all kinds of little awards here and there in the art game, but nothing like that, nothing with the celebratory people singing. I'm not used to that. It was a great evening and a lot of nice people came."

Of course, the night was not without its humor. "We are here to pay tribute to one of America's great artists," Freddie Roman announced. "A man who has combined sports, art, and entertainment in a way that has never been done before. And done brilliantly. All done without a paintbrush—his mustache created all of these images. Imagine that."

Mickey Freeman's comments that evening were also pretty much on par with what's expected from the Friars.

Lucie Arnaz was the mistress of ceremonies at Cy Coleman's in-house salute—1996

Geraldo Rivera appears to be taking calls from Don Imus during his Friars Club salute but that's not really the case. Although nobody remembers at this point who the hell they were taking to — 1976

"LeRoy is not like these abstract artists. He makes paintings—they're people, you can see faces," Freeman said. "An abstract painter is a man who paints on canvas and then he wipes his brushes off on a rag, and he sells the rag. That's what happened to Picasso. Picasso was accosted by some kind of a maniac, and the police asked if he could make a picture of the assailant and he did. Two hours later the police arrested the Eiffel Tower, a nun, and a pushcart."

Pat Cooper had a field day playing with Neiman's name. "Leonard Nemoy—whatever the fuck his name is—a man who they call 'the rainbow painter,'" Cooper said. "I got a painting of LeRoy Nemienien's of Muhammad Ali standing over Sonny Liston, and I can't find Sonny Liston. And they call him a fuckin' genius. Leroy Neminen, if you know him personally, he's a bore. He contributes nothing but boredom, but he gives great boredom."

When Cooper was through, it was Neiman's turn to take the stage. His comments were short

Lee Roy Reams, Don Pippin, Billy Stritch, Florence Lacey, Jerry Herman, Carol Channing, Jack L. Green, Alix Corey, Laurie Beechman, Leslie Uggams, and Ruth Stern pose for the Friars' standard "group shot" on the winding staircase at the Friars salute to Leslie Uggams — 1994

and sweet: "I don't feel qualified to say too much after Pat Cooper. When you sat at the table with all these comics, Milton Berle and all these people, it was downright humbling because you just didn't dare to say anything funny—you couldn't."

Susie Essman shares another memory of these

Jean-Pierre Trebot emphasizes that there have been a number of interesting people and events held at the monastery, away from the maddening crowds of hotel ballrooms. "We've certainly had a fascinating mix of personalities standing on our makeshift stages," he says. "You'd see Freddie Prinze joking for Billy Eckstein at one event, and Leslie Uggams honored at another. Tiny Tim is strumming his ukulele for an all-star night, and at another Liza Minnelli is singing for Billy Stritch. Nathan Lane is ribbing James Naughton while Paul Newman laughs his head off.

"I've attended book signings that have run the gamut from a classy evening for opera great Jan Peerce's autobiography, to a diet book party where young waiters and waitresses wore nothing but fruits and vegetables strategically placed on their bodies. Richard Belzer's book about conspiracy theories was very popular, but so was Soupy Sales's joke book. What other club would consider entertaining its members with an old-time carnival sideshow where someone eats light bulbs, walks on broken glass, and puts rubber balloons up his nose to pull it out of his mouth? If you take a step back and think about it, I suppose to some it's all incredibly insane. But while you're in the moment it's absolutely wonderful. There is no other place like the Friars when it comes to the scope of variety one finds by just walking through our doors."

Susan Lucci is thrilled to have been part of this eclectic grouping, having been feted with an in-house salute. "Everyone was very nice to me, unlike a lot of the Roasts," says Lucci, who admits she was a bit concerned that the salute would turn into more of a Roast. "I don't know whether it's because the Friars, early on, were much nicer to women, but it was a very casual evening. I do remember Rudy Giuliani, and his then-wife Donna Hanover, presenting me with flowers and saying nice things. That was a huge honor. I know one way or the other, whether they roast the daylights out of you or say nice things, it's an honor. The Friars Club honoring you is great." The Friars wouldn't want *All My Children*'s Erika Kane pissed at them, that's for sure.

"I did a salute to Buddy Hackett and after that Buddy asked me to open for him," says Judy Gold. "I opened for him a few times, and we went to the Concord to do a big fundraiser. We were backstage and he goes, 'Give me a kiss,' so I give him a kiss. He goes, 'No. Tongue.' I go, 'Eeeewww!' Because of the Friars Club I got to work with the most amazing people. When you become a comic you just never think you're going to be on the same stage as them. Buddy called me at home; I still have his number in my Palm Pilot."

A ROOM BY ANY OTHER NAME

Various rooms throughout the monastery have been named after famous Friars. Among them are

Donna Hanover and NYC Mayor Rudolph Giuliani present Susan Lucci with flowers at the Friars salute in her honor—1994

Billy Crystal and Robert De Niro analyze why in the world the Friars named a bar after Billy—2003

the George Burns Room, William B. Williams Room, Milton Berle Room, and, of course, the Joe E. Lewis Room. Frank Sinatra, the master of the house, can lay claim to the main dining room, and the newest room honor goes to Billy Crystal.

"Billy has a great respect for the history and traditions of the industry," Freddie Roman says. "I think he's quite touched that we named the room after him. He's just a wonderful, wonderful guy. The picture that he wrote, *Mr. Saturday Night*, is a perfect example of how he loved the tradition. The character was based on Berle, and Alan King, a lot of Gene Baylos is in there. He just loved all of that tradition."

At an event held at the club to cut the ribbon, Billy and a few of his friends—Robert De Niro, Bob Costas, and Joe Torre among them—partied in the Billy Crystal Room. The fact that Crystal doesn't drink, and his room is the main-floor bar, is typical of the Friars' offbeat sense of irony. "Billy is the only one who has a room named after him who is still alive," noted Alan King.

Of his room, Crystal said, "Well, now I can officially say, 'Two Jews walked into a bar. . .and named it after me.'"

Pat Cooper, who worked with Billy in *Analyze This*, also tells a story of being at the ribbon-cutting party: "You know what I told Billy Crystal? I said, 'You know, Billy, off the record, between us, I turned it down.' He went, 'What?' I said, 'Shh, don't say nothin', Billy.'"

LEADERS OF THE PACK

Being an organized institution with a formal board of governors, the Friars Club has its own political structure. The Friars even hold annual meetings and cast their ballots for the board. Everyone votes, even Pat Cooper—although he disputes this, in spite of his moment in the voting booth being caught on camera. "You know something?" he says. "I didn't vote. I said, 'I ain't gonna give nobody my vote.' Who the fuck knows? I pressed buttons. I'm lucky I didn't blow up the building!"

Cooper may mock the voting system, but it actually has been in place for a hundred years.

Pat Cooper votes for a new board of governors and hopes they're funnier than the previous administration—1990s

"We have our own who's who when it comes to board members down through the years," Trebot explains. "Our abbots have been great leaders in entertainment, so it stands to reason they should lead the Friars successfully. George M. Cohan, George Jessell, Milton Berle, Ed Sullivan, Frank Sinatra, and, of course, Alan King have helped steer us into the new millennium. But there have also been the deans of the club. In recent memory, Harry Delf, Buddy Howe, William B. Williams, Jack L. Green, and Freddie Roman have worked side-by-side with the abbots to make sure we open the doors each day."

Holding the Friars' most prestigious position means a lot to Alan King, to whom Frank Sinatra passed the torch. "When Frank was ill and they asked me to take over, I said, 'Only if Frank calls.' And he did. I still have the letter that he wrote. It's very formal: '…and the mantle is being passed on to you and your responsibilities.' It was a

Top left: *Joe E. Lewis at his* The Joker Is Wild *book party — 1954* Top right: *Joey Adams signs copies of his book for composer Mitchel Parish at Joey's book warming — 1975* Bottom left: *Opera great Jan Peerce signs his book* Bluebird of Happiness *for Joey Adams at his book warming — 1977* Bottom right: *Joy Behar gets laughs out of Danny Aiello and Susie Essman during her book warming for* Joy Shtick *— 1999*

Richard Belzer's book warming for UFOs, JFK, and Elvis, Conspiracies You Don't Have To Be Crazy To Believe In *brought in some of his friends — Alan King, Danny Aiello, (Belzer), Jerry Orbach, Gilbert Gottfried, Paul Shaffer, and Joy Behar — 1999*

very sweet little letter. At the bottom in hand—the letter was typed—it says: 'P.S. If anybody gives you any trouble, call me.'"

King's duties are not to be taken lightly. "I take it very seriously. Especially when you get to my age, it's tradition. I've been here for so long, more than half a century, so I feel, in a sense, an obligation. The Friars Club has been very important to me. It's the glue that held all of us kids together; I watched all the great stars that preceded us. Oh, there was backbiting and bullshit like anything else. There were different camps, and everybody would fight

with everybody else. Nothing changes in clubs. But it was full of shit."

Although he spends his life making people laugh, Dean Freddie Roman also takes his duties quite seriously. "My son called me when he found out I was elected and he said, 'My God, that's really an achievement. To be the president of a club that's the most fabled in entertainment,'" Roman says. "And it was. It was very impressive for me. It's been a wonderful ten years. I've enjoyed every minute of it."

Jack L. Green held various offices on the

"Over the Brooklyn Bridge" with Elliot Gould, Robert Merrill, David Susskind, Howard Cosell, and Sid Caesar – 1984

board, but being named dean was his crowning achievement. "The night I was elected I sat down and I said, 'Wow, look at this. I remember coming here and having my ham sandwich as the lunch special, and now I'm running this club,'" Green says. "I say 'running' because our abbot at that time lived in California. Although we did talk a lot on the phone, he was not available to be here all the time. So, in effect, I was here—and I felt a tremendous responsibility. It was up to us to make it go and run, and we ran through bad economic times for a while. And we just had to boost it and make it work, and it worked."

There are also a few other key players in the "making-the-club-run-smoothly" department. Under each dean is an executive director. Throughout the years, they've helped keep the club running like a well-oiled machine. Carl Timin, who started when the club was housed in the Edison building, and Walter Goldstein, who succeeded him, are to be commended for their contributions as executive directors in making the Friars the success that it is. Current Executive Director Jean-Pierre Trebot has brought the club into the trendier era, guiding the club on its wacky journey toward its centennial. He has encouraged and seen the inclusion of women as members; oveseen major renovations to keep the building functioning in a modern world, while keeping the fabric of simpler times intact; and played a large role in putting the Friars into the TV spotlight with their televised Roasts on Comedy Central.

It can't be easy managing a place overrun with comedians—and men. The club's current prior, or vice president, Sally Jessy Raphael can attest to that. "I don't know how I got to be prior," she says. "I was always a little suspicious of that, but I think I represent four minorities, so that's a classic. I'm female, Christian, Hispanic, and Buddhist." For Raphael, being an officer of the club is an important role. "I have flown in just for these meetings from wherever I am. You want officers to be there, and you want them to care. When you sit there as prior of the board of governors and you watch Alan King talking and you watch the guys—usually there aren't any women there. When I started, Ruth Stern was the only woman, and then Joan Rothermel. There's never been more than one other woman since I've been there. So one keeps quiet and listens to 'male think', and it's pretty interesting. It's my only chance to hear that. I tell you, I'm married, but if I were a single woman I'd join this club."

It doesn't take much for anyone to realize that the Friars Club is really the joke capital of the world, as Sally can attest: "They asked me if I would chair a board of governors' meeting, so I got out *Robert's Rules of Order*, and I read it because no one ever asked me to chair anything except a bar stool." Which, by the way, is true. On many of the chairs throughout the club are nameplates for various Friars. At the

second-floor bar are several bar stools, and two of them have nameplates—one for Señor Wences and the other for Sally Jessy Raphael. Don't even ask why or how those two names made the barstool grade. Maybe Señor Wences was also a Buddhist.

Sally continues her story about the board meeting: "I was very serious. I thought, 'Oh my God. I've been asked to run a meeting, and look—there's a long table, and there's like twenty-something people on it with nameplates.' Oh, thank God for the nameplates! After I did all the Robert's rules, which is the reading of the minutes and all that business—and they gave me a gavel, which is sort of like being Judge Judy—the first order of business was: Do we want to license our name to a chicken company for Friars Fryers? I read it and I thought, okay, this is somebody's joke because I'm taking over.

"Then I realized that it was real because I looked up at Jean-Pierre and he wasn't smiling or anything. So he must have meant that I put that

Sam Waterston, Jerry Orbach, and Dick Capri at the Friars in-house salute to Jerry—2000

out, so I put it out. And then I listened to twenty-five minutes of chicken jokes. Every chicken joke that has ever been told. By then it was seven o'clock and the meeting is supposed to be over because whoever is in the theater has to go. I thought, nowhere in *Robert's Rules of Order* does it ever say anything about listening to twenty minutes of chicken jokes. Then I went home and silently said a prayer: May Alan and Freddie always be in town, because I don't want to take over one of those again."

The "sunshine committee" was created in the mid-sixties by a group of Friars who worked in the garment district. Their intent was to collect and distribute toys and clothing to needy children, to make their holidays brighter. One committee member, Buddy Clarke, says, "I was one of the originators of the wrapped toys and parcels for distribution at Christmastime. We'd spend hours on a Sunday wrapping packages." The event evolved into an annual holiday party, treating 1,500 underprivileged and disabled children each year to a movie and goody bags filled with toys, candy, and items they normally don't have access to, like hats and scarves, tooth brushes, and socks. Doling out the bags are celebrities such as Michael Spinks, heavyweight boxer, and Rod Gilbert, New York Rangers hockey player. Even Milton Berle and Frank Sinatra played Santa for the kids. The Friars also send clowns to entertain residents at children's homes throughout the year.

Today the sunshine committee, which is headed up by Tom DeBow, Joe Gelber, and Philip Baird, has expanded its mission and is devoted to helping other groups in the community. For instance, the committee sometimes sends comedians to perform at senior citizens' centers. This group of Friars is just one example that shows that the club is not all about dirty jokes and puff pastry.

Sally Jessy Raphael and her husband, Karl Soderlund, are regulars at the sunshine committee's holiday events. "The Friars do good things. I've always shown up for the kids at Christmas," she says. "One year I had to walk. We had a blizzard that day, so Karl and I walked from where we are uptown all the way over to the movie theater. We felt like the Vikings by the time we arrived there. It's special to see the kids, and it's special to give them the gifts."

Stewie Stone is a driving force behind the sunshine committee's entertainment activities. "I'm involved in the shows and coming up with ideas to raise more and more money," he says. "That's the best thing I can do because that's where my expertise is." The Friars do have a serious side when it comes to charity—they just don't want too many people to know about it, lest they lose their bad-boy standing.

MEMBERS ONLY

A crowning moment for any Friar is when he or she receives the Friars Club pin. It happens at a special induction ceremony for all new members, and while there is no secret handshake to learn or any standard Friars joke to recite, it is a nice event for Friars to meet and greet their new fraternal buds. Along with the pin, members can purchase other Friars Club items that offer a rush like that one that comes from wearing a varsity jacket. Throughout the years a few celebrity Friars even have modeled for the brochures. Where else can you find Frank Sinatra, Susan Lucci, and Jerry Lewis sporting the newest Friar fashions?

In 1975 the monastery went Hollywood when they filmed a scene for *The Sunshine Boys* with George Burns and Walter Matthau. The two Friars

NBC Weatherman Al Roker is presented with a Friars Club Award by Freddie Roman at his in-house salute—2000

were right at home: Matthau played cards and Burns smoked his cigar. "It was both exciting and boring at the same time," says Jack L. Green. "I don't have to tell you about making a film; you watch them twist a doorknob for three hours 'til they get the right move. But it was exciting being around it, and it made the club even more a part of show business at that time."

Jean-Pierre Trebot recalls Matthau arriving for the shoot that day: "The minute he got here he asked if we had a poker table. Oh, man, did we have a poker table? We had a beautiful old one, and they brought it down to the second floor where they were filming so Walter could play between takes. He loved that table so much he asked if he could buy it from us. But then he found out the cost of shipping would have been exorbitant, so he changed his mind."

From day one these good ole boys could always drop by the club for a shave and a haircut. Today the barbershop is still open for business. "The second Tuesday of every month I go to Luigi for a pedicure and a bikini wax," jokes Jeffrey Ross.

Joy Behar agrees that the barbershop is worthy of a few zingers: "I don't think of it as a beauty salon, frankly. If you walk into the room, it doesn't exactly scream beauty. It's like *Cheers* for the geriatrics set—everybody knows your blood type."

In spite of any reservations Friars a few decades back had regarding letting "furriers" in, today they are the perfect complement to the entertainers. The comedians have a built-in audience and they can't ask for a more accepting, albeit tougher, crowd, a topic on which Stewie Stone is something of an expert. "They love comedy here and they appreciate it, but they're tough because they have heard everything and they know good," he says. "They love when you ad-lib with them. Somebody once told me that being a comic is like being a lion tamer: An audience smells fear. When you go in that lion's cage and you're scared, it smells fear—and that whip and that chair ain't gonna scare it off. If that audience feels that you're afraid of them, you're in a lot of trouble, and you learn here not to be afraid of an audience. They may be richer than you, they may be more successful than you, but it's your stage, and you plant your feet on that stage and you own it. We never die here. If you die, you're afraid to show up for the next fourteen days. If you died in a show, you're afraid to have lunch—you lost weight because you didn't come back in this place to eat for two months."

"They've seen everything. They know everyone," Susie Essman says of the Friars who are regulars at club events. "At the same time, they're a great audience for the same reason, because if you're good and you make them laugh, they appreciate you like no one else is going to appreciate you. They're absolutely a tough audience. I don't know if they're jaded so much as just overexposed—they've seen it all. But that's one of the good things about being a woman. They haven't seen a lot of women comics over the years and that's more of a novelty to them—especially a woman with a mouth and an attitude. They're in a state of shock, especially these old guys. They're, like, staring at me. They don't know whether they want to fuck me or laugh at me. It's all so confusing to them," she laughs.

The Friars are a unique, free-thinking, sometimes wacky, often crazy (in an endearing way, of course) bunch of individuals who have differing opinions on everything from how to tell a joke to what condiments go best on a brisket sandwich. But there is one thing they do agree on: their affection for the Friars Club. Taking them back to a fourth-grade essay question, ask these members, "What does being a Friar mean to you?" and the positive responses are endless.

"It means an acceptance into the fraternity," Freddie Roman says. "Helping to carry on a tradition of show business that's now a hundred years old in the setting of a fabulous club. The people that love this club, they show up for every event we run. Events that, when I hear about them, I say, 'Nobody is going to come to this,' and then 120 people show up and we're sold out. These people, especially the people not in show business, support every activity. They're the lifeblood of the club, really, in terms of economics. For me to be the president of all of this is just wonderful, and I can't tell you the pleasure I get from it."

Judy Gold says, "It means I belong to this great, incredible society of entertainers, and it's like a dream come true. I could not wait to call my mother to tell her that I was a Friar. It was like getting my Ph.D., basically, in entertainment."

Jerry Stiller says, "It's an honor because I'm on the same page as some of those other people who were the greatest of our generation. They were able to change your thinking. This was a religion—comedy. It was so great that they didn't have to get in front of a pulpit and start to hammer you with homilies and parables. They made you laugh, and that laughter released you from all of the pain that you had. I don't get up in the morning and say, 'I'm lucky to be a Friar,' but just to hear you ask me these questions in some way puts me into this place. It honors me."

Susie Essman says, "Being a Friar means to be a part of a legacy of great entertainers that I'm proud to be a part of—that I'm very touched to be a part of, actually. The fact that Frank Sinatra signed my certificate when I first became a member is just—I mean, Sinatra! It's really cool."

For Stewie Stone, being a Friar is about sharing a fraternal bond. "You're never going to be alone," he says. "If my wife is away somewhere I can come here and there's always someone to have a cup of coffee with, have lunch with, have dinner with. I know if there's a problem I can call the

News kingpins Gabe Pressman, Mike Wallace, and Walter Cronkite relax for a change at the Friars in-house salute to news legends—2002

Friars and there will always be someone there to help me. If, God forbid, I die and the worst fear of my life was having an empty funeral, I know that there will always be people to come because it's the Friarly thing to do.

"As a Friar I worry about my fellow Friars. I worry about my fellow performers. You're never alone in life; you're never alone in death. They don't forget you. We still do jokes about the comics that passed, we still talk about them with reverence and love. We joke about them—we still call them bad names, which means they're still alive in our hearts and our minds. That's what being a Friar is. You never leave us."

Jan Murray cites the social aspect of the club as a highlight of his membership. "What interested me was that there was a place like the Friars where actors could communicate, where they could have fun together," he says. "You take three comedians and put two doctors and a lawyer at the table, and suddenly it's not that funny because you're trying

to make them laugh. But you put six comedians at a table and we have the best time in the world. We die laughing, because if a guy gets hot, we lean back and listen to him and enjoy it. We're not going to say, 'Geez, I've got to try to top him because the fucking doctor isn't laughing.' To me, that was a very important function that the Friars had and what interested me most. That's why I try to help whenever I can, to keep a place like that alive."

Joy Behar agrees: "You go in there and everyone is like, 'Hi! How are you? You look good! You've lost weight!' There's a certain camaraderie. The people who are involved in the Friars are all committed to comedy and making people laugh. It's not a club for policemen; it's a club for funny people who make fun of the drooling and make fun of death and old age—and that's the thing that I appreciate about it. That it's fearless. You have people who have possibly just gotten a diagnosis, and yet they're laughing about it. It's the greatest thing. You can't beat it!"

Ed McMahon says, "It's one of the biggest honors of my life to be invited to join this elite group. I fashion myself as an entertainer, and here are the great entertainers of the world gathered in one organization, and their primary purpose is to please people and to entertain. I'm so fortunate to be considered notable or valuable enough to be one of them."

Jack L. Green says, "There were a lot of great things that happened in this club through the years. Things that people talk about, things people don't talk about. It is just being around the club and watching it evolve, and also watching the history of show business evolve around this club. I saw the Bilko

James Naughton and Friars Club Executive Director Jean-Pierre Trebot make things happen at Naughton's Friars Club salute—1998

series the other night. Well, all the people in the Bilko series used to be here for lunch every day. Kojak, I used to bring Telly Savalas in for lunch and we'd have cocktails here, and when he was in New York shooting the show he spent a lot of time here at the club. It's where your business and your social life intermingled and it was one."

Norm Crosby says he wants to be sure the legacy of the club continues: "What happens when all of those people who know the history die out? There was one old Indian who knew all the history of the tribe, and he would teach it to somebody younger so that over the years, there was always somebody in the tribe who knew the old stories—of how the sun came, and the moon, and where the earth came from. We don't have that in the club. There will be a day when nobody really remembers. Write it!" Okay, okay, done!

Jean-Pierre Trebot says he is celebrating the club's centennial by looking toward its bicentennial: "The Friars will be around for the next hundred years. They have to be—we just placed a time capsule into the building that will be opened in 2104. I suspect that a group of funny Friars, drinks in hand, will toast the Friars of the first hundred years with a few salty comments and a heartfelt thanks for the memories."

The Friars express wonderful memories of their time in the club. And while not every picture and every story can be shared, there will always be someone, somewhere talking about those jovial

Soupy Sales throwing his trademark pie in Pat Cooper's face. Soupy's antics around the monastery are legendary and his "Stop Me If You've Heard It" joke nights are a Friars Club staple that is not to be missed!—2001

Friars. For LeRoy Neiman, there's something special about just entering the monastery. "I just think—approaching the building, either coming from Park Avenue or Madison Avenue—when you approach the building you always see a couple of the guys going in there, slowly making it up the stairs. There's something special about it. It's not like going up the stairs to the Plaza or something, but there's something special going up the stairs." Of course it's special—it's the Friars Club, one hundred years young.

FRIARS FACTS

Milton Berle and Joe E. Lewis — 1953

Alan King — 1961

Ed Sullivan — 1972

ABBOTS 1907–2004

1907	WELLS HAWKS
1908	CHARLES E. COOK
1909–1911	JOHN W. RUMSEY
1912–1919	GEORGE M. COHAN
1920	JOHN L. GLEASON
1921–1926	GEORGE M. COHAN
1927	WILLIAM COLLIER
1928–1932	GEORGE M. COHAN
1933–1935	GEORGE JESSEL
1936–1938	JAY C. FLIPPEN
1939	ELIAS SUGARMAN
1940–1945	MILTON BERLE
1946	MIKE TODD
1947–1953	MILTON BERLE
1954–1955	JOE E. LEWIS
1956	MILTON BERLE
1957–1971	JOE E. LEWIS
1972–1974	ED SULLIVAN
1975–1996	FRANK SINATRA
1997–PRESENT	ALAN KING

TESTIMONIAL DINNERS

1907	CLYDE FITCH
1908	VICTOR HERBERT
1908	OSCAR HAMMERSTEIN
1908	JOHN RUMSEY
1908	JOHN DREW
1910	WILLIAM HARRIS
1910	GEORGE M. COHAN
1912	IRVING BERLIN
1913	DAVID WARFIELD
1916	ENRICO CARUSO
1918	AL JOLSON
1920	MARY PICKFORD AND DOUGLAS FAIRBANKS
1922	KENESAW MOUNTAIN LANDIS, WILL HAYS AND AUGUSTUS THOMAS
1924	NELLIE REVELL
1925	CALVIN COOLIDGE
1925	ALFRED E. SMITH
1926	ARTHUR "BUGS" BAER
1927	JIMMY WALKER
1928	FRED BLOCK

Buddy Howe presents Joey Bishop with his testimonial dinner award — 1964

Kirk Douglas is honored to be honored by the Friars — 1977

Barbara Walters as the Friars Woman of the Year is congratulated by her Mistress of Ceremonies Candice Bergen and Freddie Roman at the Friars testimonial dinner in her honor — 1994

1932	JOE CUNNINGHAM
1935	JAKE LUBIN
1950	JOE E. LEWIS
1951	JACK BENNY
1952	FRIARS FROLIC
1953	BOB HOPE
1954	GEORGE JESSEL
1955	DEAN MARTIN AND JERRY LEWIS
1956	ED SULLIVAN
1957	PERRY COMO
1958	MIKE TODD–FRIARS FROLIC
1959	STEVE ALLEN
1960	DINAH SHORE
1961	GARRY MOORE
1962	JOE E. LEWIS
1963	MILTON BERLE
1964	JOEY BISHOP
1965	JOHNNY CARSON
1966	SAMMY DAVIS, JR.
1967	STEVE LAWRENCE AND EYDIE GORME
1968	ED SULLIVAN
1969	BARBRA STREISAND
1970	TOM JONES
1971	ALAN KING
1972	JACK BENNY AND GEORGE BURNS
1973	CAROL BURNETT
1974	DON RICKLES
1975	WALTER MATTHAU AND GEORGE BURNS (THE SUNSHINE BOYS)
1976	FRANK SINATRA
1977	KIRK DOUGLAS
1978	DAVID BRINKLEY, WALTER CRONKITE AND HOWARD K. SMITH
1979	JOHNNY CARSON
1980	BUDDY HOWE
1980	DR. HENRY A. KISSINGER
1981	BURT REYNOLDS
1981	BUDDY HACKETT
1982	CARY GRANT
1983	ELIZABETH TAYLOR
1984	WILLIAM B. WILLIAMS
1984	DEAN MARTIN
1985	MILTON BERLE
1986	ROGER MOORE
1987	RED BUTTONS
1988	BARBARA SINATRA

Johnny Carson is loving his Friars Oscar — 1979

David Brenner and Joan Rivers get chummy at Richard Pryor's Roast — 1991

Metropolitan Opera star Robert Merrill opened many Roasts and dinners with the Star-Spangled Banner, and he is featured here opening the Drew Carey Roast in 1998

1989	ALAN KING
1990	DIANA ROSS
1992	CLIVE DAVIS
1993	NEIL SIMON
1994	BARBARA WALTERS
1997	JOHN TRAVOLTA AND KELLY PRESTON

CELEBRITY ROASTS

1949	MAURICE CHEVALIER
1950	SAM LEVENSON
1951	PHIL SILVERS
1951	HARRY DELF
1951	MEL ALLEN
1952	LEO DUROCHER
1952	ROCKY MARCIANO
1953	SOPHIE TUCKER
1953	MILTON BERLE'S BACHELOR LUNCHEON
1953	EDDIE FISHER
1954	RED BUTTONS
1954	MARTHA RAYE
1955	HUMPHREY BOGART
1956	SAMMY DAVIS, JR.
1957	JOE E. LEWIS
1958	RED BUTTONS
1959	MILTON BERLE
1959	JIMMY CANNON
1959	JACK E. LEONARD
1960	GEORGE BURNS
1960	JOEY BISHOP
1961	LUCILLE BALL
1961	ALAN KING
1962	JAN MURRAY
1962	JOHNNY CARSON
1963	STEVE LAWRENCE
1963	JACK BENNY
1964	JACK CARTER
1964	NAT "KING" COLE
1964	SAMMY DAVIS, JR.
1965	MARTY ALLEN AND STEVE ROSSI
1965	SOUPY SALES
1966	AL KELLY
1966	MAYOR JOHN V. LINDSAY
1967	MILTON BERLE
1968	EARL WILSON

Drew Carey was thrilled to receive his Roast Award — 1998

At his Roast, Ernest Borgnine takes one on the chin from the champ, Michael Spinks — 1988

Legendary Roast staples Jack Carter and Norm Crosby — 2000

1968	HARRY BELAFONTE
1968	DON RICKLES
1969	JACK E. LEONARD
1970	DAVID FROST
1971	PHIL SILVERS
1971	PAT HENRY
1972	ED MC MAHON
1973	HENNY YOUNGMAN
1973	HOWARD COSELL
1974	GEORGE RAFT
1974	MILTON BERLE
1975	REDD FOXX
1976	TELLY SAVALAS
1976	JOEY ADAMS
1977	TOM JONES
1977	TOTIE FIELDS
1978	NEIL "DOC" SIMON
1979	ROBERT MERRILL
1979	NORM CROSBY
1980	GEORGE STEINBRENNER
1980	PAT HENRY
1981	JIM DALE
1982	DICK SHAWN
1983	SID CAESAR
1984	ROGER GRIMSBY, CHUCK SCARBOROUGH AND ROLLAND SMITH
1985	PHYLLIS DILLER
1986	JERRY LEWIS
1987	RICH LITTLE
1988	ERNEST BORGNINE
1989	BRUCE WILLIS
1990	CHEVY CHASE
1991	RICHARD PRYOR
1992	BILLY CRYSTAL
1993	WHOOPI GOLDBERG
1994	BOB NEWHART
1995	STEVEN SEAGAL
1996	KELSEY GRAMMER
1997	DANNY AIELLO
1998	DREW CAREY
1999	JERRY STILLER
2000	ROB REINER
2001	RICHARD BELZER
2001	HUGH M. HEFNER
2002	CHEVY CHASE
2003	TOM AND DICK SMOTHERS

Lionel Hampton playing his signature vibraphone at his Applause Award dinner — 1998

Harry Belafonte with Morgan Freeman at Belafonte's Applause Award dinner — 2000

Betty Comden and Adolph Green perform at their Applause Award dinner — 2001

FRIARS FOUNDATION APPLAUSE AWARD RECIPIENTS

1982	ABRAHAM D. BEAME
1983	ARMAND HAMMER
1984	STEPHEN WYNN
1985	WILLIAM B. WILLIAMS
1986	BERNARD MYERSON
1987	JACK L. GREEN
1988	SAMUEL J. LEFRAK
1989	DAVID B. CORNSTEIN
1990	LOUIS WEISS
1991	LEO JAFFE
1992	SAMMY CAHN
1993	FRANCES W. PRESTON
1994	TONY BENNETT
1995	FRANK MILITARY
1996	TED TURNER
1997	JOHN KANDER AND FRED EBB
1998	GERRY GRINBERG
1998	LIONEL HAMPTON
1999	DWAYNE O. ANDREAS
1999	ALAN KING
2000	ROWLAND SCHAEFER
2000	HARRY BELAFONTE
2001	JACK TEICH
2001	BETTY COMDEN AND ADOLPH GREEN
2003	MURIEL SIEBERT
2003	CY COLEMAN